This Year a Pogo Stick . . .

NEXT YEAR A UNICYCLE!

My Journey Through Life and the Advertising Business

JIM KOBS

RACOM COMMUNICATIONS
Chicago, Illinois

Copyright © 2011 by Jim Kobs

Editor: Richard Hagle
Cover and interior design by Sans Serif, Inc., Saline, MI

Published by:
Racom Books/Racom Communications
150 N.Michigan Ave.
Suite 2800
Chicago, IL 60601
312-494-0100 / 800-247-6553
www.racombooks.com

All rights reserved. Printed in the United States of America. Except as permitted under the United States Copyright Act of 1976, no part of this publication may be reproduced or distributed in any form or by any means, or stored in a database or retrieval system, without the prior written permission of the publisher.

ISBN: 978-1-933199-30-6

Contents

Contents

Introduction

I still don't have a Unicycle. But I do like this book title. It occurred to me when I included a Pogo Stick on a recent Christmas wish list. I like trying new things.

In just the last few years, I've dabbled at drawing . . . took guitar lessons . . . started juggling . . . zoomed down a high-speed slide at a water park . . . done a little cooking . . . and signed-up for an acting/improv class. The more things you can do, the more choices you have of how you spend your time. And the more choices you have, the more opportunities you have to do something you really enjoy.

Does that strike you as rather philosophical? It should. Because this introduction will explain why I'm writing this book and what I hope to accomplish with it. Plus give you a little preview of what's included.

There are a lot of reasons for writing an autobiography. All of us want to be remembered. Putting words on paper provides some permanence. Maybe even a feeling of immortality. Or leaving a legacy.

For me, it's also a chance to look back on a wonderful life. A life that now seems to have zipped by rather quickly. One day your whole life is ahead of you. Next thing you know, you're looking in the mirror, wondering who that old guy is.

Cicero, the Roman philosopher, recorded his thoughts in what later became a book titled *A Life Well Spent*. My life probably has not been spent as well as it could have been. Yet I like to think I've experienced some things that are worth passing along to future generations. Not just stories and memories collected the past seventy years, but lessons and advice. Some people refer to this as an *ethical will.* The theory is that you should leave your family with your values as well as your valuables. A regular will provides for the orderly transfer of your property and possessions. An ethical will tries to transfer the intangibles. So expect to hear about my beliefs, morals, and feelings—as well as my hopes and wishes for my loved ones.

For some reason I've always been a saver. I'm literally surrounded by papers, files, journals, books, pictures, and memorabilia. Some things go back over fifty years to when I was in college. I now realize that I'll spend the rest of my life trying to clean-up this stuff . . . but I won't get done.

What was valuable enough for me to save, will be less valuable for my kids.

As Eric Zorn pointed out in his *Chicago Tribune* column: "Our paper trail degenerates with each generation," meaning: each generation saves a little less from its ancestors. So that's another reason for writing this book: Hopefully it will outlive my folders and files.

Finally, I've always been somewhat creative and liked to write. Over the years I've written many articles, papers, and speeches. A few might be worth saving. And this book will be a handy place to preserve some of them. Plus, I've kept a diary since 1972, which should be a good memory jogger.

Now it's time for a quick preview of what the book will include.

Here's my life in a nutshell: Born in Chicago. Wasn't a very healthy kid. But was pretty smart. Shy guy goes to college. Discovers advertising and girls. Marries wonderful wife. She raises three great kids. I work hard for others. Finally get my own ad agency. Sell it for big bucks. Later pushed out by my protégé. Form an agency/

consultancy. Grandsons start adding up. Time to semi-retire. Deal with health issues. Think about what to do next.

That's quite brief. I'll go into a little more detail in the chapters that follow and cover a few other topics. Hope you find it to be a good read.

Jim Kobs

1

All Shook Up
Putting Things in Perspective

"HIT THE BRAKES" my brain screamed to my body! After years of driving, you react instantly when you suddenly see another car crossing in front of you. But at the same time, you know it's too late.

My wife, Nadine, and I were on a two-lane, county highway in rural Wisconsin. Her Rejoice Choir had a singing date in Green Lake, where one of the choir members had a summer home. We were looking forward to a weekend of fun and fellowship. It was Saturday, July 7, 1990. I was driving, she was dozing.

Someone had told us to avoid the expressway and take local roads. It seemed to be working out pretty well. There wasn't a lot of traffic, so we were sailing along at or near the state speed limit and hadn't seen a traffic light or stop sign for miles. But there was a stop sign coming up. And I never saw it.

An older-model car was crossing the intersection in front of us.

The woman driver had three female passengers and thought she had the right-of-way. She did. The stop sign was on our road, not hers. We smashed into her car at high speed.

Suddenly our car was spinning around in circles. The air bag in the steering column had inflated, so rapidly I was barely aware of it. By the time our car had spun off the road, the air bag had totally deflated.

My first concern was for my wife in the seat next to me. She had stopped screaming and started sobbing. Our Mercedes didn't have an air bag on her side, but we both had our seat belts on. One of the car's safety features was that the seat belts automatically tightened upon impact. The result: Neither of us got a scratch . . . even though the front end of the car was badly damaged.

Wish I could erase my memory of the next couple hours . . . the sight of a badly injured young woman hanging out of the other car . . . the seemingly endless wait for the ambulance . . . police officers asking questions . . . cars slowing down or stopping to see what happened.

A lot of nice people helped us get through the not-nice situation. A police officer told us there had been other accidents at that intersection and that they were looking at ways to make the stop sign more noticeable. Somebody drove us back home to Illinois. We told a few family members and friends about the accident and asked them to pray that the women in the other car would survive and recover.

How quickly things change. Only a few days before the accident I had been notified that I had won the Ed Mayer Award for education excellence from the Direct Marketing Educational Foundation. It's one of the top national awards in the direct marketing field. I was the youngest recipient to date. And I was looking forward to the award presentation at our October convention in San Francisco.

At age 52, I had already achieved a good deal of business success. I had built Kobs & Brady into a leading direct marketing ad agency. I was making good money while I owned it; then became a multimillionaire when I sold it. Would it all be lost in the accident settlement?

The next few days were full of mental anguish. I tried to sort things out and find out how the people in the other car were doing. The accident was clearly my fault. How had I missed that stop sign? Had my negligence killed someone?

The only phone number I had was on the business card a police officer had given me. I tried calling the police on Sunday. They didn't know anything yet and told me to call the hospital. The hospital wouldn't give out any information to a non-family member.

We finally found out on Monday, two days after the accident, that only one woman in the other car was critically injured. Her name was Marjorie. She was a 28-year-old teacher who had been riding with her mother, sister, and aunt. As the week went on, we learned that Marjorie was expected to live. But she had spinal cord damage and would be paralyzed for life. We continued to pray for her.

Our car was towed back to town so we could clean out our stuff and get repair estimates. The insurance company tried to repair it, thinking almost all the damage was to the front end. Later they found some major problems under the hood and totaled the car.

I called our lawyer, who agreed to work with our insurance company's legal staff. He felt the financial consequences could be substantial but probably wouldn't wipe us out or cause us to lose our home. That was a relief.

Things slowly got back to normal: work . . . seeing family and

friends . . . going to ball games. Baseball has always been my favorite sport. But the outcome of today's game doesn't matter much when you've just flirted with life and death.

Over the next few months we learned that Marjorie eventually had been released from the hospital. She lived on a small farm with her husband and was confined to a wheelchair. Her husband didn't want to spend the rest of his life with a paraplegic and filed for divorce.

Our court date was set and later postponed. My lawyers met with the lawyer Marjorie had hired. They were asking for a substantial settlement to cover a lifetime of medical care and lost wages. The amount was way in excess of the liability limit of our auto insurance policy. Ironically, I had applied for an umbrella liability policy a few months before the accident and been turned down.

My main lawyer strongly recommended we settle out-of-court. He said a court case in a small Wisconsin town would paint me as the bad guy. The jury would see me as a big city, rich guy speeding through town in his expensive Mercedes and almost killing an innocent young neighbor.

We took his advice and had him negotiate the best settlement he could get.

It was a multimillion dollar figure that represented about one-fourth of our total net worth. We signed the papers and gave them a check in December 1990.

The lawyers handled the whole thing. We never met or talked to Marjorie. However, we did get a nice thank you note from her sometime later.

Looking back on what happened, the accident and settlement helped me put things in perspective. You realize how important life is. How quickly things can change. And how suddenly you can lose the nest egg you've worked so hard to build. In January 1991 we met with an estate-planning expert. We set up trust funds for our three kids and started each of them with a substantial cash gift.

As scheduled, I received the Ed Mayer Award at the DMEF's convention dinner in October, 1990. Nadine was there . . . along with our son, two daughters, and a son-in-law. I worked hard on my ten-minute acceptance speech. It was a careful blend of gratitude and humor, plus a serious message. It closed with the following personal note:

I recently went through an experience that shook me up quite a bit and made me realize how fragile life is. You never know how many days or years we have left on this earth. So if there's something important you've been thinking of doing or haven't done lately, don't wait too long to do it.

Maybe that's why I decided not to delay writing this autobiography any longer. So let's go back to the beginning and see how things started for me.

Lessons Learned: This might get a little preachy before I'm done. But I said in the introduction that I want to pass along some things I've learned. The accident story has some pretty obvious ones: Pay attention when you're driving, always wear seat belts, and protect yourself financially with umbrella liability insurance.

2

Early Years
The Little Professor

I don't know how many taxi drivers there were in Chicago in 1938. But on Monday, June 27th, when Fred Kobs, flagged down a taxi to take his pregnant wife to the hospital, he happened to get the same driver who had taken them to city hall for their wedding the previous August.

That unlikely coincidence brought me into this world. And a few days later, Mom and Dad brought me home. Home was a third floor apartment they shared with my Mom's mom at 1729 N. Halsted in Chicago. They didn't own a car. Or really need one. Most family and friends lived within walking distance. The neighborhood grocery store and butcher shop were only a few doors away. We could walk to more shopping . . . or even to Lincoln Park.

The apartment was long and narrow. In the kitchen there was a small stove that burned wood or coal. A larger, oil-burning stove was in the dining room. The living room and front bedroom over-looked Halsted Street. That was my bedroom for a while. Down below, Halsted was one of the major city streets. This was before busses, so street cars provided public transportation. They rumbled along day and night. The stuff on my dresser would shake when one went by. Visitors would remark about the noise, but we got used to hearing it.

From what I've been told, there were two important traits that I developed in those early years. One was a fondness for reading. My children's books were read to me so often that I practically memorized them. If the reader accidentally skipped a word or page, I knew the story well enough to correct them.

Apparently, I was also neat and organized. If someone played with my toys or books, I expected them to "put it like it was." (My toys are bigger and more expensive now, but I still expect others to return them the way they found them.)

My brother, Bob, was born when I was five. We were different from little on: I was slim; he was chunky. I was the shy, book-worm type; he was personable and outgoing. I think I was about six when my grandma died. My sister, Diane, was born two years later, when I was almost eight. My cousin, Eleanor, also lived with us for a while . . . until she was old enough to get her own apartment. By that time, our apartment was getting rather crowded. El and I slept together on a fold-out couch in the living room.

We have a lot of baby pictures of me because my Dad was work-ing as a commercial photographer. Some of them make me look like I was cross-eyed. We went to an eye doctor. My right eye had *ambly-opia*, which is commonly called *lazy eye*. He put a patch over my good eye to force me to develop the bad one. I was supposed to wear it 12 hours a day. But I was already in grammar school, and I couldn't read that way. So I would loosen a corner of the eye patch and sneak a peek with my good eye. Maybe that's why my right eye never developed. Or maybe we started too late. But before long, I was permanently wearing glasses.

Another problem developed in fall 1944, when I was in first grade. I was going to Newberry School, just a couple short blocks from home. I came down with rheumatic fever. Back then, before penicillin and antibiotics, children would sometimes get rheumatic fever after a strep throat. The rheumatism-type symptoms included swollen knees and fingers. The standard treatment was bed rest. My report card shows I missed 22 days that semester, over 4 weeks of school. Little did I know that rheumatic fever would be much worse the next time I got it.

Other than those first-year absences, grammar school was a breeze for me. I got almost all E's for *Excellent* and was double-promoted twice—once in the third grade and again in the fourth. They didn't have advanced classes back then. If you were doing well, you got double-promoted and skipped a half-year.

I'm convinced that my early reading really paid off. (If you can read well, most of your other subjects become easier.) We learned to read phonetically. I remember one class where the teacher would call on you to stand up and read aloud. You kept going until you made a mistake. Other kids might stumble after a few sentences or paragraphs. I could sometimes read a whole chapter or two without an error.

Other than school, I went to St. Michael's Catholic Church for a weekly catechism class and made my First Communion there. I was shy and introverted, though I did have a couple of boy friends. We'd go to the nearby Boys Club after school, where I took a photography course and we played a little ping-pong. But most of our sports activities were in the streets or school yard.

Two baseball games were popular, depending on how many kids were around. One called for using chalk to draw a strike zone on the school's brick wall. We'd use a pink rubber ball and take turns pitching, batting, and fielding. If only one or two other kids were around, we'd use the school stairs for stoop ball. The batter would throw the ball at the stairs and try to hit an edge . . . which would usually make the ball sail over the fielder's head.

I also heard a lot of swear words from the older kids who sometimes hung around the school yard. I had no idea what they meant. When I was being punished for something, I'd have to sit in the dining room behind the oil stove. I'd mumble some of those swear words at my mother under my breath. Luckily, she never heard me because her punishment could be quite severe.

I always looked forward to dinner time. Not because of eating. We had a radio near the kitchen table and supper time was when many of the kids programs were on. Like Tom Mix, my favorite cowboy. He was sponsored by Ralston Cereal. If you sent in a box top and ten cents, you could get cool premiums . . . like a ring with a hidden compass. Sure wish I had saved mine.

Fond Memories: Playing a table-top baseball game with my Dad and Uncle Herman. We played it so much that we wore out the cardboard parts, and my Dad made metal replacements. Also, people celebrating in the street down below when World War II ended. And visiting my Uncle Ed's family, who lived near Lincoln Park.

3 Years on the South Side

When I was 12, our landlord wanted our apartment for a relative, so he raised our rent. I think it went up to about $30 a month. My Dad was working as an electrician at the time and could probably have afforded the increase. But he always loved nature and saw an opportunity to move to the suburbs.

We moved in with a cousin in Oak Lawn who had recently lost her husband. She had a ranch house at 9817 S. McVicker. It was on a double lot with plenty of fruit trees. There was also a fenced-in chicken shed in back, which was ideal for a dog. My Dad's brother, Uncle Ed, was raising German Shorthair Pointers at the time, and he gave me one. Her name was Freda.

Since he could no longer take the street car to work, my dad got his first car and I got my first two-wheel bike. I also exhibited some early entrepreneurism. I answered an ad to sell magazine subscriptions and hit on the relatives. But it was no fun cold-calling on strangers. So I paid my brother to go door-to-door and collect old magazines. The mailing labels would show when their subscriptions were due to expire. So I could call on people a couple of months before and offer to renew their subscriptions.

The move meant I had to go to a new school to start the eighth grade. It was probably an adjustment because I was getting mostly B's and C's to start the school year. But I finished the year with all A's and earned a nickname as *the little professor.* On June 6, 1951 I was the valedictorian at the Simmons School graduation ceremony. My one-page speech thanked the school officials . . . and especially all the parents "for their help and encouragement."

The nearest high school was in Blue Island, where I spent my

A volunteer visited La Rabida on weekday evenings, and drew this sketch of me

freshman year. The following year I was in the first class at Oak Lawn's new high school. In February 1953 I got rheumatic fever again. I was bed ridden at home for about six weeks and not getting any better. So about April 1st (some joke) I was admitted to La Rabida Sanitarium on Chicago's South Side.

They specialized in treating kids with rheumatic fever. I was pretty sick when I was admitted. So I was confined to bed for over two months and given aspirin every four hours around the clock. Unlike most kids, I had visitors every day. My Mom took a street car, subway, and a bus to visit three days a week. My Dad had a second job then but would come two nights a week and bring my brother and sister on weekends. Kids weren't allowed to come inside, but I could see them from my window.

By June, I had improved enough to spend a little time out of bed. This was gradually increased, while the doctors monitored my continued improvement. We had a few celebrity visitors, including Joe Garagiola, a catcher who had just been traded to the Chicago Cubs. I became friends with a fellow patient, Gary Stoddard. We had a lot of fun together before we were discharged, especially finding excuses to visits the patients in the girls' area. However, after five months at La Rabida, I was certainly ready to go home.

My Aunt Frieda had vowed to write me a letter *every day.* She called it "Operation Letters." Letter number 113 was written on September 11 and headed *Mission Accomplished.*

Back to the North Side

Home wasn't the same one I left five months earlier. That summer our cousin had sold the Oak Lawn house and moved to the Northwest side. She bought a two-story house at 5617 N. Miltimore. We moved along with her, and rented the main floor. I was supposed to start my junior year of high school at Taft, but it was a mile walk, with no busses. Since we lived only a few doors from Milwaukee Avenue, which did have busses, I was able to get a health permit to go to Schurz. It was my third school in three years, but at least I started with one friend who went there—Gary. And through him, became friends with Ron Clayton. Both friendships have continued for over fifty years!

Ron's house was a favorite after-school hang-out because it was just a block North of Schurz. Bob Jebelian was another good friend. We'd often spend Saturdays at a park near his house, where I learned to play tennis. I was still quite introverted, so I didn't get involved in many school activities. Or do any dating.

It took me a while to adjust to a new school again. My junior-year grades were only a little better than average. I took two courses in summer school and had better grades my senior year. The typing class I took was a big help in college. My graduating class had about 360 kids, and I just barely ranked in the top fourth.

Looking back on my early years, I was lucky to have great parents . . . two of the world's nicest people. Our family wasn't wealthy, but we always ate well and had nice clothes. I only have a couple negative memories. One was when I overheard my Dad say he liked my brother, Bobby, better than me. It came after a few drinks at an uncle's house. I know Dad didn't mean to hurt me, but obviously it made enough impact that I still remember it about sixty years later.

Fond Memories: Going to Springfield to watch Schurz win the state baseball championship in my senior year. Going to a Bears game with Gary at Wrigley Field; back then, you could buy tickets at the gate before the game. Getting a new tape recorder as a Christmas gift and recording family members. Also vacations in Wisconsin, where my Dad helped Uncle Herman build his cottage . . . and we kids got to discover the great outdoors.

Lessons Learned: The importance of religion. I went to church regularly, and when we lived on Halsted Street, I even had an altar on my dresser. Cheating with the eye patch taught me a valuable lesson about following doctor's orders. I did so at La Rabida and went back there for annual check-ups for many years.

3

College Days
Coming Out of My Shell

Should I stay or should I go? I had finished my classes for the day and was debating whether to head home, but I had heard there was a meeting of the Social Science Club that afternoon. I walked over to the meeting room and stood outside. *Should I stay or should I go?* I was nervous and afraid to go in.

At the same time, I was determined *not* to remain the shy, introverted guy who had gone through high school with few friends and no dates. Wright Junior College was a chance for change: a new place where nobody knew me.

I finally got up the courage to go inside. A small victory, perhaps. But as you'll soon see, the college years were where I really came out of my shell. Before long, I was involved in all sorts of new activities and started developing leadership qualities.

When high school ended, my Uncle Ed got me a summer job in

the mail room at Hotpoint. I sorted mail in the morning and delivered it in the afternoon . . . from the factory area to the executive offices. The executive offices were much more appealing. Little did I realize that I'd spend most of my career creating advertising mail. Fact is, I didn't have any definite career ideas at that time.

So I started at Wright looking for a career. Thought about becoming a lawyer. Tried a couple business and accounting courses. Even took a speech class to help overcome my shyness. It worked, but it wasn't easy. I recall standing behind the podium with my legs shaking and my knees knocking. I leaned on the podium with my elbows to steady myself. Fortunately, my voice didn't give way to my nervousness, and my speeches got good feedback.

One thing lead to another. I took more speech classes, including one on debate. Wright didn't have a Debate Club, so I started one and was elected president. I also joined the International Club and was chosen to be on the Student Senate. I headed a couple of Senate committees and eventually wrote a new Constitution for the Student Governing Body.

My speech classes began to pay off when the Social Science Club held a mock Democratic political convention in April 1956. About a thousand students took part. Mayor Richard J. Daley gave the welcoming address. Serving as the Democratic National Chairman, I followed his speech with one of my own. I traced the history of the Democratic Party . . . blasted the Republicans for their shortcomings . . . and called on the delegates to "write a new chapter in America's political history."

As a freshman, my grades were good enough to make the Dean's Honor Roll. The following year saw the formation of a Phi Theta Kappa chapter, the national honor society for junior colleges. I was

Now you can attend college by way of television's Channel 11. Think how important a college education can be to you. How much more prepared you would be to raise a family. How much more valuable an employee you would be.

TV College makes it so convenient that it is no longer necessary for anyone to be without a college education. No need to leave the family or travel to school after a long working day. You attend Chicago City Junior College in the comfort of your home. And you choose from accredited courses in Business, English, Mathematics, Humanities, Psychology, and the Sciences. These courses are so planned that they can lead to an Associate in Arts degree, evidence that two years of planned college work has been completed. Should you wish to go on with your education, you can transfer these credits to other colleges and universities.

And no wonder, the TV courses are conducted almost like classroom courses. A regular class schedule is followed, with the courses televised for half-hour evening sessions. Most of the courses "meet" only three times a week, yet you receive full college instruction and credit. And the most popular courses are also televised in the afternoon, when they may be more convenient for busy mothers.

While watching, you have a study guide handy, making it easy to follow the instructor. If you're taking the course for credit, you do the assignments in your study guide and mail them in to your assigned teacher. They are graded and speedily returned to you. When examination time nears, some of the courses have review discussions to answer your questions and prepare you for the exam. The exams themselves are given at the branch of the Chicago City Junior College nearest your home. That's all there is to it. After completing the course, your grade is mailed to you and credit for the course is put on your permanent record card. (Special examination arrangements are made for hospitalized or seriously handicapped students.)

As a student of TV College, you can use all the services provided for the classroom students of the Chicago City Junior Colleges. The branches have excellent library facilities. In addition, trained counselors are on hand to help you choose a vocation and find a worthwhile position.

So why delay your college education any longer? TV College makes it possible to get that education at low cost. Remember, anyone regardless of where he lives can take the courses *without credit*, the only cost being a $1.00 charge for each study guide. If you live in Chicago and have graduated from high school or are over 21 years of age, you can enroll in TV College *for credit* at the low cost of $5.00 for a part-time program or $10.00 for a full college program. Students who don't live in Chicago may take the courses for credit by paying tuition in addition to these service fees.

That's how easy it is to get all the advantages of a college education in your own home. But, you don't have to take our word for it. Last spring and fall, more than 8,000 credit and non-credit students enrolled in TV College. Here's what some of them had to say:

"... *My classes have brought new interests into my life, and in doing so, have made me a better mother and a better citizen.*"

"... *This is indeed a splendid opportunity for us 'older' folk who had no chance to attend college.*"

"... *I have found the courses to be very well presented, interesting, challenging, and meaningful.*"

Why not plan now to let television help you receive the benefits of a college education.

This Advertisement Prepared by Students of Wright Junior College and appears as a Public Service Feature by Polk Bros.

"Education by TV is now a proven reality. It offers equal opportunity for adult education to everyone, and therefore makes an important contribution toward strengthening our American heritage. The rewards you receive will benefit not only you, but your whole community."
—SOL POLK, *President, Polk Bros.*

THIS SEMESTER THE FOLLOWING COURSES WILL BE OFFERED:

Accounting	Humanities	Physical Science
Biology	Mathematics	Shorthand
English	Psychology	The Slide Rule

You can enroll for credit at any of the five branches of the Chicago City Junior College on Monday, Tuesday or Wednesday, September 9th, 10th or 11th at 10 A.M. or 6:30 P. M.

For complete information on TV college and its courses, just fill in the coupon below and mail it today.

---- FREE INFORMATION ----

TV COLLEGE
Department C,
3400 N. Austin Ave.,
Chicago 34, Illinois

Please send me further information on TV College and its courses.

NAME...

ADDRESS...

CITY... STATE.....................

The ad that launched my advertising career.

one of the charter members chosen by a faculty committee, and elected Treasurer at the first business meeting. Despite all my activities, I graduated with a 3.9 average, which placed me fourth in a class of 341students.

But my big break came the semester before graduation, when I took an advertising class. Chicago's PBS channel had just launched a TV College that allowed students to take credit courses at home. As a public service, Polk Bros.—the city's leading appliance dealer— donated a full-page ad in the *Chicago Tribune* to promote the program. Our advertising class competed with those at other Chicago City Colleges to create the ad that would appear in the newspaper.

A group of judges chose the ad from my class as the winner. It was headed: **"TV Brings College into Your Home."** A committee of 15 students had worked on the ad, but I had written the headline and most of the copy. It was the first of many successful coupon ads I would eventually write. And it also resulted in a job offer!

College Interrupted by My First Advertising Job

Little did I know that Polk Bros. was looking for a copywriter to join their advertising department and write copy for their many newspaper ads.

I was excited by the opportunity. However, it was a full-time job, and I intended to enroll at the University of Illinois that fall. So I took the job . . . under false pretenses. I intended to treat it as a summer job and resign after a few months. But I had a nice boss who took a liking to me. My ads were appearing in the city's four newspapers on an almost daily basis. I was also learning a lot about the retail advertising business.

Meanwhile on the home front, my folks were about to buy a new home in Glenview. I had learned to drive the previous summer, when I worked with my Dad as an electrician apprentice. And I was now making enough money to buy my first car . . . a used Ford sedan.

So when it came time to enroll in fall classes, I didn't. The decision was not popular with my parents. They felt that I'd get used to a regular paycheck and never finish college. I insisted I would only work for a year.

It turned out to be a very interesting year. The first six months were spent at Polk Bros. on the Northwest side. I took three advertising and marketing courses in night school. Then right before Christmas, the whole staff was told Polk would be closing its advertising department and giving their account to a former ad manager who was starting a new agency in the Loop.

His name was Jack Pettersen. It would be his decision to make: Which four or five staff members would he take along to join Jack Pettersen & Associates? Fortunately, my boss and I were chosen as the print advertising team. That meant we continued working on Polk's ads, as well as a few other clients that were added later. We even did a little direct mail advertising. It was my first taste of working in downtown Chicago.

The year went by pretty quick. It was enough to convince me that advertising would be my career. Also, I realized that I preferred the agency side of the business more than the client side.

Preparation for an Advertising Career

Going to the University of Illinois in Champaign-Urbana was quite a change from junior college. I was one of about twenty thousand students. I lived in a dorm my junior year. A great corner room with two room mates. One was a freshmen who much preferred dating to studying. We sometimes double-dated.

My first date was with a cute freshman from Kankakee—Nancy Crosby. It led to my first serious relationship; we continued to date off and on until after I graduated. But my best date was the very lucky night when I met my future wife. Nadine deserves much more than a brief mention here. So I'll save her for the family chapter.

I majored in Advertising, which was part of the Journalism School. I applied for a scholarship that offered the winner a neat choice: $500 or a part-time job with a local ad agency. I won it and took the job. It mostly involved clerical work, but I did get to write a few ads for a local bank.

I also joined Alpha Delta Sigma (ADS), a professional fraternity for advertising men. The initiation was fun. Pledges had to convince one or more local stores to buy an ad on a sandwich board. We would create the ads for them and carry the boards around campus for a day . . . one hanging in front and one in back. I got the prize for raising the most money from my ad sales.

After my experience at Polk Bros., my advertising courses really seemed easy. One that proved to be especially valuable was a course called "Sales Writing." It was actually about writing direct mail. The instructor was delighted that I later entered the field, and we remained friends until he retired.

When my junior year ended, I went back to Polk Bros for a summer job. I was hired as a salesman in their Garden Shop . . . selling mainly lawn mowers. I quickly learned the spiff system. Polk's sales tags only showed the list price. Customers knew they had to ask for the "Polk price." We knew how low we could go, and if we got a higher price, we would earn a bigger spiff or commission. By the end of summer, I was the top salesman in my department.

The money helped me pay my way through college. But I knew I couldn't afford to stay in the dorm another year. So I moved to an independent house for my senior year, where I got what was known as a meals-and-table job. There were two of us. We served breakfast, lunch, and dinner to the other students living in the house. We also did the dishes and cleaned up after dinner. Instead of having a dorm room upstairs, the kitchen crew studied and slept in the basement . . . in an open area next to the ping pong table. I was elected House President.

On October 7, 1959, as we were finishing the dinner dishes, I got a *bad news* phone call. My sister had been killed in an accident. It was a long ride home for the wake and funeral. It was a devastating loss for my folks. Having your child die before you must be one of the toughest things a parent can endure. Unfortunately, our family had to suffer through another fatal accident 13 years later. My brother was visiting a friend in Florida. The camper his friend was driving on the morning of January 2, 1973, tipped over as he made an abrupt turn, and Bob was killed.

My senior year was the last chance to get involved in extracurricular activities. I sold ads for the school newspaper, *The Daily Illini*. There was also a campus radio station, WPGU. I had my own afternoon DJ show three days a week, where I played "The Tops in Pops." It was so much fun I briefly considered a radio career.

But my first love was writing. One of my courses was Narrative Writing. It was a good chance to do a story about advertising. At that time, there was a best-selling novel, *The Man in the Gray Flannel Suit*. An equally popular ad campaign was built around women, with headlines like: "I dreamt I went to the opera (or other such events) in my Maidenform bra."

My parody was titled *The Man in the Gray Flannel Underwear*. Somehow or other the publisher of *Chaff*, a campus humor magazine, heard about it. Before long, it became my first published work. I sent a copy home. My Mom said she laughed out loud a couple times reading it. The story is in the Appendix.

In April 1960, a female ad student and I were selected as the outstanding U. of I. seniors to attend the Advertising College Awards in St. Louis. We spent three days visiting local advertisers and media. It was my first airplane trip.

Before wrapping-up my college years, I should interject a few personal notes. Appearance-wise, my height and weight were average. I looked studious and collegiate with a crew cut and glasses. I started smoking a pipe at the U of I . . . a habit that I continued for almost fifty years.

I had a lot more friends in college than I ever did in high school. But I was still somewhat insecure and retrospective. I clipped a lot of articles from magazines and newspapers. And kept a journal of sorts. I still have a few pages headed "Observations of a Rambling Mind." It begins with "I shall attempt to discover what I need and want most in life, and determine a sensible plan on how to reach it."

As graduation neared, I did some job interviews. I was disappointed that only one ad agency came to campus for interviews. It was a major Chicago agency. My interview went well enough that they asked me to complete a detailed psychological questionnaire. I was hoping for a job as a copywriter. Instead I got a turn-down letter.

At least the agency shared the analysis of my test with me. It suggested copywriting was not the best career choice for me. However, it described me as a "serious, intent young man . . . with determination to achieve and excel." It concluded that I was so highly motivated that I could probably succeed at whatever career I chose.

I graduated in June, 1960 in the upper 5 percent of my graduating class, and was one of five students to receive an award from Sigma Delta Chi, the professional advertising fraternity.

Fond Memories: Football Saturdays at the U. of I. If we didn't go to the game, we could interact with the crowd going to the stadium from our dorm window — complete with a loudspeaker and background music. Also doing my own radio show, where I could play pop tunes, kid around, and do a shout-out to my friends.

Lessons Learned: You *can* turn your life around if you're really determined and work at it. I made a lot of progress in college, but still wish I had a few *do overs*. There were some attractive girls I was too shy to ask out . . . only to learn later that they would have gone out with me . . . if only I had asked. To get an acceptance, you have to risk getting a turn-down.

4

Wife and Family
I'm Glad You're Mine!

"I've got us a couple dates, but they're nothing special." That's what Nadine's friend told her when she came for a weekend visit to the U. of I. early in November 1958. But that blind date led to a special marriage. And a special family with three great kids and, at last count, eight wonderful grandsons.

I don't remember too much about that Saturday night date. We probably went to the Tumble Inn, an off-campus hang-out where you could have a few beers and sing along with the piano player. Something must have clicked. I knew I wanted to see Nadine again.

So I picked her up on Sunday morning to show her the campus. One of the female dorms we walked past was near a wooded area. It was pretty quiet. We stopped and kissed. I'd never been kissed like that before. It wasn't a nice-to-know-you peck on the cheek; it was warm and wonderful. We kissed again a few hours later . . . before

Nadine hopped on the train back to Chicago. But I didn't let her get in the train before I got a phone number and made plans to see her when I got home.

Looking back, I really lucked out. I was average-looking at best. Nadine had a pretty face, lovely smile, nice legs. In other words, she was beautiful. Still is, over 50 years later.

When I wasn't in school, I was living with my folks in Glenview. I usually came home for a weekend visit every few weeks. Nadine lived with her folks in Villa Park. My old Ford put on a lot of miles going back and forth between Glenview and Villa Park.

Back at the U. of I., we stayed in touch with letters and occasional phone calls. I also exercised my creative talents by sending homemade cards. I still have more than thirty letters that Nadine wrote in the year-and-a-half before I graduated. They document how rapidly our relationship grew serious. Here's the close of her January 4 letter, only about two months after we met:

> *I almost forgot to tell you about the robbery here. Some thief stole my heart. It was last seen in the vicinity of Villa Park, but it's rumored the thief plans to take it to Champaign. If you come in contact with the thief, tell him to handle with care. It's a very delicate heart and needs lots of love. Bye for now, honey. I love you. Nadine*

The letters also reflect the concerns of our growing relationship. Her religion has always been very important to Nadine, and it bothered her that she was falling in love with a Catholic. We talked about it off and on and finally agreed that if we got married in my church, she could raise the children as Lutherans. The courtship continued after I graduated. On Christmas Eve, 1961, I popped the question and slipped a ring on her finger.

A number of Nadine's friends were getting married at about the same time. We especially liked Jan and Jim Van Ewyk's wedding. So we pretty much copied it. That meant a reception in the Bensenville fire house . . . with lunch meat sandwiches for dinner . . . and a great band that kept the dance floor full.

My cousin, Frank, the only one in the family with a movie camera, filmed both outside the church and at the reception. We borrowed another movie camera from the Van Ewyks and flew to Las Vegas the next day to start our honeymoon. From there, we drove to Los Angeles, then North to San Francisco. Before heading home, we flew to Seattle, and spent our last week-end with a former U. of I. classmate, Fred Cappetta and his wife.

Our first apartment was a one bedroom on the third floor near Madison and Central. It was the far West Side of Chicago. The main attraction was the location at 5672 W. Adams Street, across the street from Columbus Park. We had one car, a new Studebaker Lark convertible, and no garage. When the winter weather dropped below zero, and the car sat on the street all night, it refused to start in the morning. So we'd set the alarm . . . I'd wake at two in the morning . . . pull on some clothes . . . go downstairs . . . get in the ice-cold car . . . and drive around the block a couple of times. Brrrrrrrrr . . . I shivered away until the engine warmed up.

Favorite newlywed story: my bride was learning to cook with the *Betty Crocker Cookbook* at her side. One night she tried a new dessert recipe. It was called a "Blueberry Buckle." She served it . . . waited patiently for me to take a taste . . . and asked what I thought. I tried to be as tactful as I could and said: "I don't know, I've never

My beautiful bride and me on our wedding day.

eaten any buckles before." I'm pretty sure I slept on the couch that night.

Nadine was still working as a secretary at U.S. Steel, early in 1964, when we learned she was pregnant. The baby was due in October. We didn't know or care if it would be a boy or girl. We just wanted a healthy baby. When Nadine went in the delivery room, I went to a nearby church to pray for her and the baby.

God answered my prayers in a very special way. Karen was born about 7:00 p.m. on October 7. It was the exact same time and date on which my sister had died five years earlier. Diane had been the only girl in our family. Now the family had a new baby girl to love, one who helped my mother get over five years of sadness, as she began to help out with babysitting.

Nadine became a full-time wife and mother. When we added a crib, high chair, and other baby necessities, our one-bedroom apartment suddenly became a little cramped. It was time to go house hunting. Fortunately, Nadine had saved enough from U.S. Steel for a down payment.

In May 1965 we bought our first house . . . a 3-bedroom bi-level at 110 Roxbury Lane in Des Plaines. It was a few years old and had a nice yard, plus a garage to keep our car warm at night. But we were warm, too. There was no air conditioning until we added a window unit in the master bedroom. My desk was in the third bedroom. I had plans to turn it into a home office.

Those plans changed in late 1967. Nadine was pregnant again, with the baby due in January. She went to see her ob-gyne doctor for a check-up in November. He told her he was pretty sure it was going to be a *multiple birth*. We soon learned we were to be blessed with twins, and they normally are born early. Not this pair. They went full term, and the doctor finally had to induce labor.

Ken and Kathy were born on January 24, 1968. Both were healthy. I felt it was really special to have twin babies. It was also a challenge when both wanted to be fed or changed at the same time. Their big sister, Karen, was willing to help, but she was only three years old. Somehow, we got through it.

Confession time: When I say we got through it, I really mean Nadine. It was early in my advertising career. I was already beginning to work long hours and do a fair amount of business travel. Thus begins the classic breadwinner trade-off. You focus intensely on work. You spend an enormous amount of time and energy to achieve corporate success. It's easy to rationalize that you are doing it to build a better life for your family.

In reality, it's an expensive trade-off. Business demands squeeze out a lot of family time. You don't intend to, yet you ignore some of your family's individual needs and dreams. Later, you wish there was a do-over that would let you go back and spend more of that precious time with your family.

As the kids got older, my work hours and travel schedule only got worse. I tried to get to as many of their school and sports activities as I could. We did manage to squeeze in a yearly family vacation . . . mostly week-long car trips that included Georgia . . . Minnesota . . . Kentucky . . . and the Ozarks.

I told the kids that when I wasn't around, they could always reach me by phone if they had a problem. But the reality is that Nadine deserves the credit for being there in person and making sure the kids turned out okay. It wasn't easy, especially dealing with teen-age growing pains. We had regular family meetings to assign responsibilities and try to smooth-out problems.

Recently, I came across some notes that Kathy made for one of those meetings. She said: "the reason Mom and Dad don't fight is he ain't home enough to fight." There's probably some truth to that.

The Family Grows-Up in Palatine

After almost ten years in Des Plaines, we decided we'd like a brand new home. We looked all over the Northwest suburbs, and finally narrowed down the choices to Palatine or Glenview. Palatine won. We moved into 245 Whitehall Drive in August 1974.

We quickly discovered one of the advantages of moving into a new subdivision: you get to know your neighbors more quickly. You borrowed tools . . . helped each other put in sod . . . signed the kids up for sport teams . . . and made lasting friendships. We still look forward to regular meetings with our Gourmet Group, whose members have become some of our best friends.

Before you know it, the kids are all grown up and have families of their own. But not without leaving some wonderful memories:

- For **Karen**, we started a family tradition on Halloween by driving her to my folks' house. We were proud when she made the high school gymnastics team. And prouder yet when she became president of her Pi Phi sorority at Illinois State. Before long, I was walking a beautiful bride down the aisle. Next thing you know, she's following in my footsteps and working in the direct marketing field. It was neat when she joined Nightingale-Conant and later became a client of my Kobs Gregory Passavant agency.

- **Ken** was always good at sports, and made his high school teams in both baseball and football. He also had a job delivering the weekly Palatine newspaper, which he did for about half of his first 14 years. I enjoyed the time we spent together in Indian Guides. Miami of Ohio was the perfect school for him. His pre-med studies led to him to a successful selling career and eventually his own distributorship. It's been great

Ken, Kathy, and Karen

to see how he built up his business and the awards he and his firm have won.

- Our little redhead, **Kathy,** seems to have grown up too fast. One minute, she was on the Fremd soccer team. Then preparing for a fashion career at Bradley. Next, she became the first family member to earn her Masters degree. She worked alongside me at KGP for a while. We once climbed Camelback Mountain together. She's dealt with some tough problems growing up, but she's battled her way through them. Every time I see her with Christopher reminds me what a wonderful mother she is.

- **Nadine** has also done a lot of growing-up since we moved to Palatine. She spent over twenty years singing with Rejoice, an interdenominational music ministry. When the kids were grown, she took up golf. Not satisfied with just doing okay, she kept practicing . . . and won the Inverness Golf Club's nine-hole Ladies Championship in 1993. Her 1999 hip replacement barely slowed her down. She still does water aerobics as many days a week as she can.

When it comes to shopping and saving money, there's none better. Likewise, for helping others: Give Nadine a needy family's Christmas list, and she'll chase from one store to another until she's satisfied they'll be happy.

In December 1987 we moved from Palatine to Inverness on the Ponds. It was time to let someone else handle the yard work and snow removal. The first dinner in our dream home was a candlelight affair eaten at a card table surrounded by boxes.

The following May, we got to repeat our wedding vows as we celebrated our 25th anniversary with family and friends. This time we were at the Drake Hotel in Chicago–not the Bensenville fire house. We had a fire engine ice sculpture to remind everyone where we had partied a quarter century earlier. It was one of many special anniversaries we've celebrated over the years.

Unfortunately, as you get older, some of your body parts begin to wear out. In 2005, Nadine was diagnosed with macular degeneration . . . and began losing her central vision. She's been getting shots in both eyes ever since, which are uncomfortable at best. Her vision has improved somewhat, yet it's hard for her to read . . . shop . . . follow recipes . . . write . . . and drive. She's had to give up or cut back on things she really enjoyed, like singing and golf. I'm extremely proud of how she's handling this difficult situation.

We've come a long way together since our first apartment in Chicago. In March 1993, we bought a home in Scottsdale. We're so fortunate that both our daughters chose to raise their families close to home in Chicagoland. And lucky that Ken's career path took him to Arizona, where we spend our winters. In December 2006, we bought a condo in downtown Chicago, which allows us to spend time in the city and enjoy cultural activities.

Best of all . . . is the added time Nadine and I have been able to spend together the last few years. Retirement is like enjoying a brand new marriage with a familiar partner. I won't say much about our love life . . . except that it started out good, has gotten even better over the years, and we still enjoy cuddling together.

Now it's time for a few words about the rest of our family. We didn't always agree with who our kids were dating. But when it came time to get serious, they all made excellent choices. We didn't know

Jim, Sophia, or Tony when they were kids. But we've seen them all grow and mature a lot as they've dealt with raising their own kids.

Dreams for My Grandsons

What a magnificent gang of grandsons they've given us! Each one is different. Each one is special. I have too many favorite memories to include them all. Instead, I'd like to share what I dream for Kevin, Ryan, Nicholas, Adam, Michael, Nathan, Dean, and Christopher. The following was written a few years ago while I was babysitting my eighth grandchild, so naturally I came up with eight dreams:

- First, that they appreciate the freedom and independence of living in America. It's a great democracy. And I expect my grandkids to vote, be patriotic, and support their country . . . whether that means singing our national anthem at a sporting event or joining the military service.
- Second, I dream they will get a good education, the kind of education a good savings program makes possible. It will open their eyes to endless possibilities and open doors in the business world.
- Third, that they will use their education to pursue a rewarding career. To me, that starts with finding a job you truly enjoy and becoming the best you can be. It might even mean starting their own business and providing jobs for others.
- My fourth dream for all my grandchildren is that they will find a spouse, who is also their soul-mate, and have a family. Only when they experience the miracle of birth will they really appreciate what loving and caring is all about.

- Next, I dream they will learn how to set goals and work hard to achieve them. I'll try to teach them the importance of positive thinking, self-confidence, and self-esteem.

- Sixth is a dream that my grandkids will always respect others. Not just their parents and authorities, but all their fellow citizens . . . whose diverse backgrounds and beliefs have enriched our culture and made America the wonderful country it is today.

- Dream number seven is that they get to travel and explore the many wonders of our world. Starting with their home states of Illinois and Arizona. This will hopefully whet their appetite to visit other states and other countries. As they do so, they'll learn a lot about other people and about themselves.

- My final wish is what every grandparent wishes for his offspring: PEACE. No more wars. No more dictators. No more terrorism. That's a lot to expect, but that's what dreams are for. And if my grandchildren don't live long enough to experience peace on a global basis, I pray they will at least find *inner peace*. For only that peace allows someone to live happily without addiction and depression. And that inner peace will allow them to enjoy all the other things I dream for them.

My closing thought is borrowed from one of our business friends, who said: "our family is a gift we gave ourselves—for 46 years the gift has grown and added richness to our lives."

Fond Memories: Going out for dinner when we lived in Des Plaines. It was usually a special occasion, like a birthday, and we'd get burgers or pizza. When the kids went off to college, I always looked forward to their Thanksgiving homecoming on Wednesday night. It's still my favorite holiday.

Lessons Learned: How important it is for family members to help out and be there for each other. I've seen all three of our kids help Nadine and me out. And I've seen them pitch-in to help each other get through some difficult situations. That's what families are all about . . . and why I'm so proud of mine!

5

Working for Others
Bosses Shape My Future

I had a lot of nice bosses in the roughly twenty years that I worked for others. Learned a lot from them. Am grateful that they all gave me a lot of independence. Enjoyed working for and with them. But my most fun boss was my Dad.

As mentioned in an earlier chapter, we spent one summer working together in the construction business. My Dad was a self-taught electrician foreman; I was a learning-on-the-job apprentice. You see your parent in a totally different way when you work together. I saw that my Dad was respected by the other tradesmen because *they* knew *he* knew his business. He was also well liked and would entertain everyone at coffee breaks and lunches with lots of kidding around.

Shift forward to Summer 1960. College was over. It was time to get a full-time job. Preferably in an advertising agency. So I used my creative skills to put together a presentation that touted my previous work experience plus my college training. Then I started calling ad agencies, answering ads, and contacting employment agencies.

An early interview was with The Rylander Company, a direct mail lettershop. Jack Thompson, a VP, was looking for a copywriter and asked me to write a sample letter for one of their clients.

It didn't sound very appealing. I didn't go to college for four years to write advertising mail! Ad agency creatives got to do newspaper and magazine ads and radio and TV commercials. However, all the agencies I talked to wanted someone with more experience. Slowly but surely, all my job leads dried up. About a month had gone by, and I was getting a little anxious.

So one morning I called Mr. Thompson at Rylander and asked if the copywriter position was still open. It was. I told him I had the sample letter done. (Actually, I hadn't even started it. I assumed he was a busy exec and would ask me to come back in a day or two.) Surprise! He asked me to bring the letter in that afternoon. I quickly started writing. And the finished project was good enough to get the job. That course on Sales Writing really paid off. I had to negotiate my starting salary with the founder, Roy Rylander, and was hired for $500 a month.

The clients I worked on were quite diverse. They ranged from well-known firms like Motorola and Seagram's to local distributors and small retailers. Creative projects were equally varied: selling magazine subscriptions . . . offering financial services . . . promoting trade shows . . . getting sales leads . . . and building store traffic. I wrote lots of sales letters, plus some brochures and booklets.

To boost response for a realtor, I recommended and wrote a *Land Buyer's Guide*. The 32-page booklet was even sold in some bookstores. When there wasn't enough creative work to keep me busy, I got to make sales calls and learn the production side of the business. Looking back, I took the job hoping to get enough experience for an ad agency to hire me. But I got hooked on direct mail and mail order and later passed-up chances to switch to general advertising.

After a year-and-a-half, one of the Rylander salesmen left and joined Combined Registry, the publishing subsidiary of Combined Insurance Company. His name was Jerry Deabel, and he soon called to ask if I would do some free-lance copywriting for them. Extra money was appealing. So I met with Jerry and his boss, Art Roberts, one night after work.

Their first assignment was to write a four-page sales letter for a new home study course. It was based on a best-selling, motivational book by Napoleon Hill. They gave me the book—*Think and Grow Rich*—for background. I only had a week for the assignment. I read the first chapter of the book and started writing the letter. I presented it the following week, and they loved it.

Art Roberts explained that they needed a lot more free-lance copywriting and that he'd prefer to work on a retainer basis rather than a project basis. It sounded good to me. He asked how much I wanted. I suggested $500 a month. He said fine. So after reading only one chapter of *Think and Grow Rich*, I had doubled my income!

What I learned from this experience was more valuable than the money. Before long, they wanted me to handle all their advertising work—including graphics, placing ads, and some production. So I got help from an art director at Rylander, plus some of their suppliers. They billed me; I marked-up their charges and billed Combined. I had my own ad agency for the first time! I dubbed it **Invest-In Advertising** and had some stationery printed.

I bought a typewriter and did all the copywriting at home, mostly late at night. I was still living with my folks in Glenview, and my "office" was the kitchen table. Client meetings were one night a week at Combined. Client phone calls and coordinating the art and production required some time during the work day. But I was careful not to steal time from Rylander. If I spent a half-hour on the phone with *my* work, I'd make sure to work an extra half-hour on *theirs*.

This went on for a full year, starting about the time Nadine and I got engaged. I didn't keep track of all the time I spent with her. But in 1962, I averaged 88 hours a month of freelance time or about 20 hours a week. Fortunately, my Rylander job was pretty much 9 to 5.

As the year wore on, I'd often fall asleep over my typewriter. You can only burn so much midnight oil before it catches up with you. Somehow I kept the client—and my fiancé—happy. But it was clearly time for a change.

W. Clement Stone and Success Unlimited

When Art Roberts offered me a full-time job at Combined, I gladly accepted and started in January 1963. The company was owned by W. Clement Stone, a self-made multimillionaire. His insurance success had been inspired by the motivational and self-help books he read. Which lead to starting his own publishing company.

Besides the home study course, we sold a number of self-help books . . . including *Success Through a Positive Mental Attitude*, which was co-authored by Stone and Napoleon Hill. There was also *Success Unlimited*, a digest-size monthly magazine. I started as the magazine's Business Manager, as well as Advertising Manager for the books and home study course.

The magazine needed improvement. The editorial content was more general interest than self-help. When I started pointing that out, the editor accused me of being after her job. She gave Mr. Stone a "him or me" ultimatum. He chose me. So I was put in charge of the magazine as Managing Director and hired a new editor. She was somewhat difficult to work with but understood what needed to be done and began to turn things around.

One night, when I was working late, a sales promotion writer for the insurance company stopped-in and asked if he could submit an article for the magazine. His name was Og Mandino. I told him we'd be happy to consider it.

The article was about Ben Hogan's golfing comeback after a bad accident. The finished article was so good we featured it as a cover story.

A few months later, I hired Og as the Executive Editor for *Success Unlimited*. He was very ambitious and eventually got Mr. Stone to put him in charge of the magazine. Og soon began writing books. His first was *The Greatest Salesman in the World*, about an ancient rug salesman who learned the secrets of selling success. The book sold very well. Og went on to become a best-selling, self-help author, and sold over 25 million books!

Meanwhile, I continued to promote the magazine and our books. Being on the client side of the business for the first time meant I got to do a little of everything . . . from creating ads and mailings to writing collection letters and analyzing results. I was also able to get more deeply involved in areas that are key to direct mail success: mailing lists, offers, and testing.

Unfortunately, we had to abandon the home study course. By early 1965, I felt we needed a new monthly continuity program that would provide a steady income stream. After interviewing a number of mail order experts, I hired Bob Stone as a consultant to help us develop and launch the product.

It took most of the year to get the product ready, prepare a business plan, and get W. Clement Stone to okay the investment. Then the product launch was abruptly put on hold. I sensed that something funny was going on and maybe I should start looking for a new job. But I waited too long. Late in 1965, all our publishing projects were cut back—and I was let go. Fired for the first time. With a wife and daughter to worry about.

For almost four years, I had been immersed in positive thinking. I had read many of the self-book books we promoted. So I knew it would turn out okay. Now I could openly look for a new job. And I decided to apply what I knew about direct mail to my job search.

The Job-Hunt Direct Mail Campaign

It turned out to be one of the most successful mailings in my career. I started by getting the membership directory from the Mail Advertising Club of Chicago. I eliminated the suppliers and selected the top exec from the agencies and users. If it wasn't obvious from their titles, I called the company to find out who the boss was.

Instead of sending a resume with a cover letter, which is too easily discarded, I decided to *offer* a resume. So those who requested one would become my job-hunt leads.

The letter I wrote not only offered my resume but also a sample of a recent mailing I had created for *Success Unlimited*. The bottom of

110 Roxbury Lane
Des Plaines, Ill. 60018
March 4, 1966

Mr. John Abrams
ABC COMPANY
Chicago, Illinois

Dear Mr. Abrams:

As a fellow member of the Mail Advertising Club, you know that experienced direct mail people are hard to come by. That's why I think you'll want to use that 5-cent stamp above to learn more about an established direct mail pro who could be <u>very</u> <u>valuable</u> to your organization.

This person has had over six years experience as a copywriter and advertising manager. He's handled hundreds of ads and mailings, with such diverse assignments as selling books and courses…getting leads for salesmen…promoting circulation and advertising…and raising funds by mail. Besides being familiar with lists, production, and analyzing mailing results – he's also had selling and management experience.

    In short, this guy <u>knows</u> <u>direct</u> <u>mail</u> <u>from</u> <u>A</u> <u>to</u> <u>ZIP</u>! As you may have guessed, The person I'm describing is myself. If you're looking for a talented, experienced mail adman, I feel I have a lot to offer. What's more, I'm preparfed to prove it with a SPECIAL FREE OFFER.

I don't expect you to thoroughly evaluate my talents by the few paragraphs above. But I'll be happy to send you an <u>interesting</u>, <u>detailed</u> <u>resume</u>. It presents my direct mail background, education, and special training, personal data, and other qualifications. Look it over and see if there isn't a place for my talents in your organization…or with someone you know.

<u>Extra</u> <u>Bonus</u>! While they last, I'll be happy to send along a "live sample" of a mailing that was recently selected by the Direct Mail Idea Library as one of the best circulation mailings of the year. You can keep this sample for your idea file – even if you return the resume!

To get the resume and sample mailing, just sign your name below and return this letter in the self-addressed envelope enclosed. Use the stamp above for postage. Or for even quicker action, you can phone me at 939-7075.

      Cordially yours,

      Jim Kobs

JK:gd

....

<u>OK</u>, <u>Mr</u>. <u>Kobs</u>, <u>Show</u> <u>Me</u>!
Please send your resume and sample mailing piece. I understand I'm under no obligation.

SIGNED_________________________________   TITLE_____________________________

( ) Check here if you would prefer to have me call you for an appointment.

The Job-Hunt Letter that produced a 20% response rate.

the letter served as a reply form. A self-addressed reply envelope was also included, with a postage stamp serving as an involvement device. A business friend had a battery of automatic typewriters. I used him to produce and personalize my mailings. I think we mailed about two hundred copies.

Then I waited for the results. They started coming quickly . . . and didn't stop. Would you believe a 20% response rate? That's what it added up to. The real sleeper was something I hadn't anticipated. Most of the respondents had a <u>new</u> position in mind—not a formal job search they had already started. So I just had to sell myself, not compete with dozens of other job applicants.

As a bonus, a couple respondents were looking for free-lance help. One of these led to a big copywriting project for Encyclopaedia Britannica. I also got four or five other free-lance projects. That meant I had some income coming in and didn't have to jump at the first job offer to come along.

To the contrary, I took my time . . . went on interviews . . . narrowed down the best possibilities . . . and weighed the pro's and con's of the final offers. It led to another job in the publishing field at American Peoples Press.

But the job search also rekindled my interest in free-lance work. One firm that needed a lot of help was Teen Mail, a co-op mailing for teen-agers. They were a steady client in 1966 and 1967, as I created their mailing inserts and promotion materials. Once again, it was time to get some stationery printed. This time I named it **James F. Kobs/Advertising** and continued to do free-lance creative work for about four years.

A Rewarding Year at American Peoples Press

My business card said I was Manager of the Mail Order Division. APP was a subsidiary of Grolier and had a mailing list of 300,000 encyclopedia owners, which was about three times the size of the database we had at Combined. I was responsible for planning, creating, and producing more than five million pieces of mail a year.

The challenge was to make a profitable mailing to our full list of customers every three weeks. Since it usually took about three test mailings to come up with one winner, we basically had to average one test mailing a week. Experience had shown we could sell a wide variety of products and services . . . including books and records . . . typewriters and luggage . . . power tools and silverware. Even big-ticket items, like organs and pool tables, were offered with free trials and monthly payment terms.

My boss was Jim Casey. He believed we had to do whatever was necessary to get the mailings out. That meant he would occasionally ask myself and our other two managers to help him unload a truck. Or if a printer couldn't start delivering our mailing pieces on time, we'd rent a station wagon and pick up enough letters or brochures to start the inserting machines.

Fortunately, I had a number of successes. Some came from creative improvements in the mailings, others from developing new offers or changing the physical format of the mailing. I also realized the importance of merchandising my accomplishments. I wrote a monthly advertising report to keep key people at the parent company aware of our promotion plans, mailing results, and what we were learning from our tests Even though it was a fairly long commute from Des Plaines to Westmont, I enjoyed the job at American Peoples Press and expected to be there a while. The "while" turned out to be only a year. On February 14, 1967, the big boss came in from New York to tell us they were closing our division. They wanted me to transfer to another Grolier division in Mundelein, which wasn't very appealing.

I quickly recalled a conversation at an advertising club meeting a few weeks earlier. Bob Stone had just opened a new ad agency, and I offered congratulations. He said they were starting to add clients and wondered if I was interested in a job. An ad agency job was still very appealing. I didn't know if he was serious or not. However, I told him I hadn't been at APP a year yet, and thought it was too soon to switch. Little did I know my job situation would change so quickly.

So I called Bob to ask if he was still looking for some help. He told me to come in and talk. I reviewed my accomplishments at American Peoples Press. I guess Bob was sufficiently impressed. He said he'd like to hire me, but they needed to finalize one more account to justify my salary.

The prospective client was in upstate New York. I knew from seeing him in action at Combined that Bob was a good salesman. He sold the prospect . . . and I had the ad agency job I really wanted!

Stone & Adler: Helping Each Other Grow

When I joined in March 1967, the agency had five other employees, plus the partners, Bob Stone and Aaron Adler. My position was a Copy/Contact job, which meant I was a copywriter who also did the client contact on my accounts. My first client was Amsterdam Company, a business mailer that sold ad specialties and printed products.

The work we were doing was direct mail and mail order advertising. It was sometimes called direct response advertising. Bob felt we should be positioned more broadly to appeal to big-name advertisers. I was at a staff meeting in 1967 where he coined the term *direct marketing*. Our stationery soon identified S & A as "the direct marketing agency."

A few months later, Bob began writing a series of articles for *Advertising Age*. I developed and edited a house organ we sent to clients, prospects, and industry leaders every few months. Our *Direct Marketing Report* included agency news and views . . . along with a client case history and an actual sample of the featured ad or mailing. The house organ went on to win numerous awards.

S & A finished its first year with 12 clients, about $500,000 in billings, and a few more staff members. I was happy to be back working in downtown Chicago and got more involved in the local Mail Advertising Club. The agency was growing—and so was I. In July 1968 I was promoted to Creative Director, but I still did account contact and worked with a variety of clients, including a leading mail order nursery.

Stone & Adler was becoming one of the largest direct response agencies in the Midwest. We were good at direct mail and catalogs, not so good at other media. So in 1971 we joined forces with a New York agency and became Rapp, Collins, Stone & Adler. That doubled our size and, the following February, I was promoted to Vice-President and General Manager. The growth of direct marketing also helped us land some blue-chip accounts.

One of my greatest success stories was with Hewlett-Packard.

They had created the first scientific pocket calculator. The HP-35 sold for $395 and was designed to replace the trusty slide rules long used by engineers. Bill Hewlett, HP's co-founder, personally approved our initial creative work. The first mailing produced about five times more orders than expected. HP sold over $100-million of calculators in less than two years, and we won a Silver Mailbox Award from the Direct Mail Marketing Association (now the DMA).

The story gets better. New products rapidly followed for both the business and technical markets. In 1974 we promoted the HP-65 as "the first pocket computer." It won the DMMA's Gold Mailbox as the best mailing of the year. I happened to be in New York when I got the news, and I was so excited I felt I could float back home without the plane. A few years later a top direct marketing expert named the Hewlett-Packard program as *the* direct marketing success story of the Seventies. Later, it was chosen as one of the top direct response campaigns of the century!

Another of my clients was Dartnell, a leading business publisher. They sold hard-bound books via mail order and sometimes offered a free booklet to boost response. I wrote a booklet for them, *24 Ways to Improve Your Direct Mail Results,* which discussed the most popular offers for consumer and business mailings. The following year I expanded it for publication by the DMMA. That checklist of *99 Proven Direct Response Offers* has become quite popular. Bob Stone even referred to it as "the standard reference for direct marketers around the world."

Bob was also busy writing. His book, *Successful Direct Marketing Methods,* was published in November 1975. Some of the staff members helped with the writing. I wrote the chapter on creating direct mail packages.

As direct marketing became more important, the general ad agencies felt they needed to add that capability. In 1976, one of the biggies wanted to acquire us, but the Chicago office had too many client conflicts. (Clients don't usually want their agency to work for two accounts in the same field.) So they bought Rapp & Collins, while Stone & Adler remained independent.

But the possible merger prompted Bob to think about Stone & Adler's future. He and Aaron were nearing retirement age. He developed an earn-out plan that called for the agency to be acquired by myself and two other VPs over a five-year period. It stipulated that the three of us were to be equal partners . . . just as Bob and Aaron had always been equal partners. I had a problem with that. I felt one of the other partners worked as hard as I did and deserved equal stock, but the other didn't. Try as I might, I couldn't get Bob to budge on this point. It bothered me enough that after ten great years with S&A, I began thinking about leaving to start my own agency.

It was tough to think about. I had always worked more closely with Bob than Aaron. We took a lot of business trips together. Bob was my mentor.

I was also well-compensated, with a $30,000 salary and $15,000 bonus.

And I had a great group of clients at that point. They included Encyclopaedia Britannica . . . Six Flags . . . U.S. News & World Report . . . and Illinois Bell. I began to wonder if any of them would follow me if I started my own ad agency.

Before long, I had a chance to find out. I was approached late in 1976 by Tom Corcoran about heading an in-house ad agency for Bankers Life and Casualty . . . one of the largest direct marketers in Chicagoland. I said I wasn't looking to join a house agency but might consider it under certain conditions. He asked me to spell out what I wanted.

We met again the following week. I gave him my conditions. I wanted to change the agency's name . . . move it downtown . . . and position it as an independent agency that had won the Bankers' account. I wanted to get outside accounts to grow the agency and eventually have a chance to acquire it. A couple of the points involved some sticky negotiations, which dragged on for a few months. But Tom and his bosses eventually agreed to everything I wanted.

The stage was set to resign. I confidentially informed a few of my accounts that I was planning to leave. I scheduled a Friday lunch date with Bob in early March, right before his annual vacation. My resignation wasn't a complete surprise. One of my clients had let it slip to someone who had passed the news on to Bob. We agreed I would work until the end of March.

The following week I let the staff know I was leaving. The rumors began flying about which accounts and people I'd be taking. Someone even suggested I'd be taking the building! So the management group panicked. When I returned from a Friday afternoon meeting, I was told to turn in my keys and leave by the end of the day.

I refused to do so. I said I had too many personal files to take home on the train that night and I would be coming in Saturday to get my stuff. The next day the building guard was not supposed to let me in, but I had worked so many evenings and Saturdays when he was around, that he didn't think I was a problem. A couple of fellow employees were there with instructions to inspect anything I was taking. They eventually got tired . . . went home . . . and left me alone to pack one file box after another with my client, speech, and sample files.

So I got to take everything I wanted. But I left with a bad taste in my mouth. I didn't think the intended lockout was a proper way to treat someone who had been a loyal staff member for almost 11 years. Later on, I had lunch with Bob Stone and patched things up. We renewed our friendship regularly . . . including yearly outings to watch the Cubs at Wrigley Field.

Fond Memories: Business trips with Bob Stone. The plane rides and after-dinner nightcaps provided a great chance to talk about everything from sports to family matters. My favorite client was Sunset House, a gift and gadget catalog in Los Angeles. S&A was about to lose the account when Bob asked me to take it over. On my first trip, I brought some creative work they didn't like. I stayed up late that night in my hotel room to revise it and presented my version the next morning. Fortunately they loved it . . . and we went on to work closely together for a number of years.

Lessons Learned: When you go into a new field, as I did at Rylander, try to learn as much as you can about it. I read trade magazines from cover-to-cover to get familiar with all types of direct mail advertising. Also, make sure you let others know what you're accomplishing . . . as I did with the advertising reports I wrote at American Peoples Press.

6

Kobs & Brady
Banking on Success

Let's start this chapter with how it ended. On September 28, 1988, there was a small party at a restaurant to mark my exit from the agency I had started about ten years before. I wasn't leaving by choice and was tempted to make some bitter remarks to the Chicago office employees. Instead, I chose to start with a few jokes, then got serious.

I pointed out that Kobs & Brady had gone through what I called "the 3 Stages of Business Growth: first, the Survival Stage . . . where you prove you can get customers, attract good staff members, provide a quality product or service, and make money doing it; second is the Building Stage . . . where the founder becomes a manager, multiplies himself, and leads the way to continued growth in clients, people, and profits.

The third stage I explained is the toughest. It's where you go beyond building a business and Build an Organization, an organization that will survive after the founder is gone. I remarked that at some point they would take my name off the door, which was okay with me, as long as the organization survived.

It certainly has. Now known as Draftfcb, it's the largest ad agency in Chicago with over eleven hundred staff members. Believe it or not, its offices now span almost a hundred countries . . . from Argentina to Zimbabwe . . . with more than ninety-five hundred total employees!

Pretty amazing. Considering we started on April 1, 1978 with Tom Brady and about a dozen people from Marshall John, the Bankers' house agency. From Stone & Adler, I hand-picked three people—my secretary, a young account exec, and an even younger assistant account exec named Howard Draft. Our office was on the 19th floor at 625 N. Michigan Avenue.

Tom Brady was a critical part of my plan. He had worked on the Bankers account for the past fifteen years . . . most recently as Marshall John's creative director. I knew him from association activities and figured he'd be a good soldier, someone I could delegate to. He was. His main job was to keep the Bankers account happy, while I concentrated on getting and supervising new business.

One thing I learned in negotiating my employment contract was there is often *one provision* that can become extremely valuable. The one I got called for a two-year finder's fee bonus for any accounts we added where I had some previous involvement. Naturally, that's where I concentrated my initial efforts. I added the first one—Stouffer Foods—before we even opened our doors. So many others followed that my bonus eventually topped-out at about $275,000.

The Illinois Bell account I had handled the last few months at Stone & Adler was one of the key ones. AT&T and its Bell operating companies were just discovering direct marketing. My Illinois Bell

Jim Kobs and Tom Brady at a K&B alumni party in 1988.

contact introduced me to her counterpart at Michigan Bell. Our first mailing for them was very successful. We eventually did work for all but 2 or 3 of AT&T's 21 subsidiaries. At one point they represented over 40% of K&B's business. When other agencies started to go after the Bell business, we hired a couple of account people from Illinois Bell to maintain our leadership.

We also added six non-Bell accounts the first year and finished 1978 with billings of $7 million. Another key account was added in our second year. I got a call one day from Jack Bishop, who I had worked with years before when he was at Sunset House. He was currently at Xerox, developing their supplies catalog. He wanted some cost estimates. A month later he called and said he was ready to go.

A few months down the road, after we had completed their first catalog, I asked Jack how many other agencies he had considered. His surprising answer was none. He said he had worked with a number of agencies over the years and never had an account executive who was as dedicated as I was. He added: "Now that you have your own agency, I assume you've hired the same kind of dedicated people." It was a thought-provoking compliment.

I like to think we did hire dedicated people. It was easier to select good additions to the creative staff because you could review their sample books. Account people were tougher . . . especially if they talked a good game. I developed my own way to find out how much they really knew about direct marketing by developing a role-playing test.

But it was still tough to identify good people for all agency departments with the usual job interview process. So we soon started using a professional testing service. Before making a hiring decision, we'd have potential hires take a series of intelligence and psychological tests. The reports proved quite helpful.

You retain good people by treating them fairly, rewarding them properly, and giving them growth opportunities. I believed that people development should be a high priority. We developed an in-house training program and an annual performance review system. Bonuses were paid to *all* staff members—not just the top execs. Kobs & Brady always promoted from within. Our continued growth gave us plenty of opportunity to do so.

From the beginning, I felt it was important to keep staff members informed about what was going on. So I started writing a monthly Progress Report. They usually included a paragraph or two on each current client . . . a review of new business activity . . . a people section that mentioned staff additions and new titles . . . administrative news . . . and activities to promote the agency. As we got busier, the reports were issued quarterly. They continued for ten years. I still have copies of all 41 reports, which have been helpful in refreshing my memory.

One of our most important staff additions came early in 1979, when Bill Gregory joined us as VP and Creative Director. He and I had worked together for about five years at Stone & Adler. Six months after I left, S&A was sold to a large, general ad agency. I sensed that Bill would be unhappy with the changes. One lunch meeting was enough to coax him into joining us.

We now had the pieces in place to continue our growth. I felt we had "arrived" that fall when we beat S&A and 13 other agencies to win the GE account. We finished our second year with $12 million in billings and almost forty people. Bankers, the house account, now represented only one-third of our billings.

K&B's growth was a combination of new accounts and new assignments from existing accounts. Xerox was one of the latter. They asked if we could sell used copiers by mail. They had a warehouse full of copiers that had been traded in. We recommended they be reconditioned and given the same guarantee as their new copiers. They went along with our recommendations and assigned us to do a mailing package. It was extremely successful. Before long the warehouse was empty, and we were selling more copiers by mail than the entire Xerox sales force!

New business was stimulated by regular exposure in the trade press. My first book, *Profitable Direct Marketing,* was released late in 1979 and promoted heavily in *Advertising Age,* the leading trade publication. I was doing a lot of speeches and seminars at direct marketing events and encouraging other staff members to do the same. Our reputation even spread overseas in 1981, when I did talks in Switzerland and London.

We also began winning a lot of awards. An ad agency has many departments, but its creative work is what has the most visibility. Bill surrounded himself with a strong creative staff. In 1981 we won two first-place awards in the local direct marketing competition, as well as the "best of show." The following year we won the most awards of any agency, and again won *the* top award—the President's Cup. I took the creative staff to the hotel bar, where we celebrated by drinking champagne from that big, silver cup.

The growth continued. Billings increased 55% in 1980 and finished at $19 million. A year later we reached $22 million. The giant ad agencies were moving rapidly into direct marketing . . . mainly through acquisitions. After only four years, we had become the largest direct marketing agency that was still independent.

Buying the Agency

Early in 1980, I had started negotiating with Bankers' management to buy the agency. Nothing much happened that year. By the middle of 1981, it looked like we had finally reached a verbal agreement . . . after months of offers, counteroffers, and arguments. Things still dragged-on. A couple of times I seriously thought about leaving and starting over. But a written agreement was finally signed on December 8, 1981. I knew it would one day make me rich.

The buy-out plan granted me the option to purchase Kobs & Brady up until June 30, 1983. The purchase price was based on a rather-involved formula. The key provision was that most of the purchase price would be paid to Bankers from K&B's earnings . . . not money I had to come up with. The sooner we reached the earnings target, the sooner the buy-out would be completed.

Before the buy-out agreement was even finalized, we began getting calls from large, general ad agencies. They were looking for acquisitions. Their blue-chip clients were requesting direct marketing expertise, and an acquisition was the most fool-proof way to add that expertise.

One of the more interesting contacts started with a phone call on November 19, 1981, from Don Zuckert, then Executive VP of Ted Bates. He said they badly needed direct marketing help on the U.S. Navy account. We did a lunch meeting the following week. Don brought along the head of a smaller agency they had acquired to underscore that they kept management in place and ran each agency autonomously.

I told him about the buy-out plan, which was then nearing completion. I facetiously explained that I thought I might get in legal trouble by trying to sell something I didn't own yet. Also, I probably wouldn't want to turn around and sell the agency immediately after completing the buy-out. However, I added that I liked their autonomy philosophy and would like to stay in touch.

Eventually we would be approached about an acquisition by nine of the top ten ad agencies. I realized that there would be some significant advantages in selling K&B. Not just a big financial pay-off for myself. But the opportunity to retain key people by giving them stock whose value would multiply when we sold.

A week after the option agreement was signed, I met with Tom Brady and Bill Gregory to outline a stock distribution plan. I proposed that when we completed the buy-out, Tom would start with

15% of the stock and Bill would get 10%. I would own the remaining 75%. I showed how their stock would appreciate from a growth in our book value over a five-year period. And I gave them a chart to show how much their stock would be worth if we sold in three to five years after we took over ownership from Bankers.

Furthermore, I explained that I didn't want to limit this profit opportunity to the three of us. I felt strongly that we needed to offer smaller amounts of stock to the four vice-presidents who were overseeing our accounts. Tom and Bill agreed. The following week I did a similar meeting with the VP's and showed what their pay-out could be from a growing book value and a potential sale.

As noted above, we had until mid-1983 to generate enough earnings to complete the buy-out. I had learned how to make money in the agency business at Stone & Adler. All K&B clients were on monthly retainers, which guaranteed a minimum income on their account. However, if the time spent on their account exceeded the retainer, they were billed for the excess. By using this system and policing expenses, we averaged an annual pre-tax, pre-bonus profit of 30%. This was about three times the industry average!

The high profit percentage allowed us to reach the earn-out target by the end of June, 1982 . . . a full year ahead of the deadline. It took another three months to complete all the paperwork and legal requirements. The closing took place on Friday, October 1, 1982, . . . just four and one-half years after K&B had opened in Chicago . . . and three days before we would be opening a New York office.

I had realized my dream to own my own agency. Now I could share the ownership with my key executives. To mark the occasion, I drafted a Declaration of Independence, which I signed along with Tom Brady and Bill Gregory.

<u>A DECLARATION OF INDEPENDENCE</u>

When in the course of business events it becomes necessary to dissolve
the bonds which have connected us with others, it seems altogether fit-
ting to declare the motivations which impel us to this separation. We,
the undersigned, having devoted our entire business careers to working
for others, do hereby announce and declare our intention to become independent by acquiring the stock and assets of Kobs & Brady Advertising,
Inc. In doing so, we are motivated by the opportunity to become free and
control our own destiny, as well as the chance for financial gains.

ASSUMPTIONS. We hold these truths to be self-evident: That under our
control we can maintain K&B's excellent reputation and continue its solid
growth record. That one + one + one = four, and the sum of our collective
experience, talents, and strengths is greater than those of any one or
two individuals. That such an effort can only succeed in a spirit of
mutual respect, trust, and cooperation amongst the three major partners.

IDEAS FOR THE NEW OWNERSHIP. That all major decisions involving the business, as mutually defined and agreed upon, can only be resolved after a
thorough discussion among the three major partners. That in establishing
authorities and responsibilities for the three partners, their strengths
and contributions shall be taken into account and an attempt made to em-
ploy each individual's talents where they will be most beneficial to the
corporation. And that in running the business the partners always be
mindful that authority is useless without the consent of the governed.

We, therefore, the undersigned, solemnly publish and declare our intention
to become independent and to mutually share the responsibilities which such
entails. And in support of this Declaration, with a firm reliance on the
protection of divine Providence, we mutually pledge to each other our Business Lives, our Fortunes, and our Sacred Honor.

Affirmed this 27th day of September, 1982

James F. Kobs

Thomas B. Brady

William W. Gregory

Kenneth Urban, Notary Public
My commission expires 7/23/85

P.S. This is serious!

Kobs, Brady, and Gregory declare their independence.

Joint Venture in New York

Our second office came about because Bates wouldn't take "no" for an answer. Their Navy account had a large direct marketing budget, and they still needed our expertise. We were interested in opening a New York office, where Bates was headquartered. There were obvious advantages in starting with a big account—as we had done with the Bankers business in Chicago.

I suggested we take a leaf from what many young couples were doing. Namely, to live together for a while to make sure we were compatible before considering a merger. Sort of a "test marriage."

We reached an agreement to do that in June 1982. It allowed us to immediately start working on the Navy account and set an October target date to open a New York office adjoining Bates. I chose Howard Draft to head the office. As my protégé, he had grown rapidly to become a vice-president and key player. He was willing to relocate. I was willing to give him a lot of responsibility. Howard did a great job in hiring staff, building client relationships, and growing the business.

The office opened on schedule in October with 15 people. Bill Gregory and I were making weekly trips to oversee things. I'm not sure it saved us any money, but the corporate apartment we added was much more comfortable than frequent hotel stays.

The Navy account was our bread and butter. But the real growth came as Bates introduced us to some of their other accounts with direct marketing needs. Before long, we were working with Prudential Insurance, DHL, and Home Box Office. The latter turned into a big account as we did mailings for their local cable operators, plus TV spots to build demand for HBO.

The Chicago office was also growing. We finished 1983 with 101 employees, 68 of them in Chicago. Over the years our combined client list included Allstate, Amoco Oil, Anheuser-Busch, Avis, Bank of America, Beltone, Colgate, Eddie Bauer, Fidelity Investments, General Mills, Harrah's Casino, Helene Curtis, Honeywell, Hyatt, Kal Kan, Life Fitness, Mars Candy, 3M, Mayo Clinic, NBC, Nestle, Nissan, Playboy, Pepsi, Perrier, Philip Morris, Pizza Hut, Polaroid, Procter & Gamble, Red Lobster, Revlon, Scott Paper, Seagram's, and the U.S. Mint . . . plus other smaller, direct response accounts. And we continued to handle the Bankers account, even though they no longer owned K&B!

Like all agencies, we had some client turnover. I felt we could minimize it if we identified and dealt with client problems. At the end of 1981, we mailed all clients an Agency Evaluation Form. They were asked to rate all our services on a scale of 1 to 5 and provide comments on how well they thought the agency was performing for their company. The forms were confidential, and returned to my attention.

It was a risky move, giving clients an opportunity to be critical. But we got way more compliments than criticism. Problems were dealt with promptly. And the total results provided a benchmark that was used to compare our ratings from one year to the next.

Besides keeping clients happy, I had a lot of other things on my plate. In 1982, I began a six-year term on the Direct Marketing Association Board of Directors. Later I served on their Executive Committee and headed a number of subcommittees. Also, I was on the Advisory Board for two firms, whose founders I knew through DMA. In 1984, my biography was added to *Who's Who in America*.

I did a total of 65 speeches during K&B's first five years, an average of one a month. In 1984, I started teaching a two-day seminar with Pierre Passavant, which I continued on my own when Pierre bowed-out. Soon after, I began teaching an undergraduate course at Northwestern University.

My time records show I was working an average of over 65 hours a week, including many nights and almost every Saturday. It was unusual if I didn't have at least one out-of-town trip a week. Sometimes two or more. I worked on airplanes. In limos. On commuter trains. Looking back, I wonder how I maintained such a schedule for more than ten years.

But I was always well-organized. I took a lot of notes and made sure they were filed. I could go from one meeting to another and quickly refresh my memory by skimming recent notes. Sometimes I went weeks before I caught up with my office mail. But I always had my secretary do a list of what was in my daily mail. So I could quickly grab something that needed immediate attention.

To minimize the time spent on administrative projects, I believed in spending the time to do it right the first time around. Especially for projects that might be repeated annually, like performance reviews. It's much easier to pull something out of a file than to reinvent it every year.

There were certainly a lot of interesting developments along the way. I was on a flight to Miami during an attempted hijacking. The hijacker wanted to go to Cuba, but we landed on the outskirts of the Miami airport. I was practically pushed out the door and down the evacuation slide. It was a little scary at the time, but nobody was hurt, and I was welcomed back to the office with a party and a sombrero. The staff memo I wrote is in the Appendix.

We often had staff parties to celebrate new accounts, anniversaries, and holidays. Family members were invited to K&B's summer picnics. I loved the annual softball games. As the boss, I could play whatever position I chose. I usually pitched and led the creative team to a number of exciting victories.

Meanwhile, the New York office continued to grow rapidly, and eventually passed the Chicago office. We tried a couple of other small offices—one in Minneapolis and another in San Francisco. Neither was very successful. However, Bates was getting some strong interest in direct marketing from their worldwide offices. I did a trip to Australia to evaluate a potential acquisition and helped train a direct marketing group in Norway.

Naturally, as we got bigger I was more involved in managing and new business than in client affairs. It was critical for account supervisors to see the big picture on their accounts, so I developed a quarterly Account Supervisor Report, which they were required to submit for each client. It provided a summary of recent activity . . . highlighted growth opportunities, along with new ideas we'd submitted . . . and listed potential problems. These reports kept me informed and trained supervisors to look beyond the day-to-day activities on their accounts.

For management matters, I did a weekly lunch with Tom Brady and Bill Gregory. We always went to a nearby restaurant. I felt that in-office meetings are usually on a tight schedule. Going out, provided a little extra time to keep everyone informed. And I controlled the subject matter by doing the agendas.

The main priorities on my agenda were to continue our growth, maintain our excellent reputation, and retain key staff members. We almost lost one late in 1984. The Leo Burnett agency went after Howard Draft with a tempting offer to head a new direct marketing division. Fortunately, he told me about the offer before accepting it. I was able to divert Burnett's attention by suggesting they could buy the whole agency, rather than just get Howard.

While they were distracted, I worked out a deal to move Howard back to Chicago and make him President of K&B. We announced his promotion in February, 1985. He began serving as chief operating officer. I moved up to CEO.

The Double Sale

This gave me more time to explore the sale of Kobs & Brady. Actually, I had been discussing the subject with Ted Bates as soon as we got the New York Office off the ground. But I wasn't in as much of a hurry to sell as they were to buy. So I purposely d-r-a-g-g-e-d things out. When I had a New York trip, I would schedule a meeting with a top Bates executive who was assigned to us. There were a lot of details to discuss. My negotiating strategy was to get one concession before moving on to the next subject.

Meanwhile, the diversionary tactic with Leo Burnett had made them a serious suitor. About the same time, we were approached by a third major ad agency—J. Walter Thompson. Even though I was very upfront and disclosed that we were close to selling to Bates or Burnett, they make us a very generous offer. The competition helped up the ante.

Overall, the trial marriage with Bates had gone well. Eventually, after dozens of meetings, I had gotten almost everything I wanted. This included 5,000 shares of Bates stock I had been promised, which would be distributed annually to K&B's management team if we met our earnings targets for the next five years. But the trade press was speculating that Bates might merge or sell to another large, general ad agency. That meant "our" Bates stock could disappear before we ever got it.

On November 13, 1983, I had lunch in New York with Bob Jacoby, the CEO of Ted Bates. I told him we were close to a deal, but I couldn't count on the Bates stock to reward and motivate our management team. He thought about it a while and then conceded. If they merged or sold after we sold to Bates, Jacoby said we should immediately be awarded *all* our incentive stock so we could benefit from their merger or sale.

The next day, I met with Don Zuckert, who was now President of Bates. He wanted a status report. I told him what Jacoby had said, and felt we were very close to a deal. Don offered to throw in 1,000 more shares of Bates stock to close the deal. I had intended to go back and review the situation one more time with my partners. Unexpectedly, I realized it wasn't going to get any better. After three years of negotiations and over a dozen file folders of notes, I had the deal I wanted. I verbally agreed to sell, if we could delay the announcement until early in 1985.

We settled on the first week in March to announce the sale. As luck would have it, *AdWeek* chose K&B as its Midwest Agency of the Year . . . with a cover story in their March 3 issue. It was the first time any direct marketing agency had been so honored by a major advertising publication. The article pointed out that "in little more than seven years, we had gone from being a direct response arm for a Chicago insurance firm to a star in the direct marketing arena."

March 4, 1986, was a busy, but historic day. We did simultaneous staff meetings in both major offices, followed by a press conference in New York. At that point, I owned 61% of K&B's stock. The remaining 39% was spread among nine of our executives, three of whom would be made millionaires by the sale. I wanted the rest of our 150-plus staff members to also get something tangible from the sale.

So Bates agreed to a unique gift program I proposed. It was designed to help familiarize our staff members with some of the well-known Bates clients. We told them they could choose one of a half-dozen, client products valued up to $500, including a Panasonic color TV . . . his and her Schwinn bikes . . . a Toro lawnmower or snow blower . . . and a 35mm Minolta camera.

A month later, we held our quarterly management meeting in Scottsdale. It was an extra reward for our top execs. One of the agenda items was a mini investment seminar I conducted. It presented some important strategies for them to consider in investing their proceeds from the sale.

Another agenda item reviewed the sale details. I suggested it might be the best orchestrated agency sale in history. I had started the agency with no investment because it was a house agency for Bankers. After it had become quite profitable, we had bought it for slightly over book value. Our success in New York had been virtually guaranteed by opening with the Navy account. I had dragged-out the negotiations for three years while Bates introduced us to other clients that boosted our profits. I then negotiated a price that was based on a multiple of our last year's earnings. A year that happened to represent a 35% growth!

But it got even better. Our sale to Bates was effective April 1, 1986. Less than 3 months later, Ted Bates sold to Saatchi & Saatchi, a giant London-based agency, in a $450-million all-cash deal. As promised, we were awarded all of our Bates incentive stock so we could benefit from their sale. I called it a *double hit.* We had already got our money from selling K&B. Now we got another big multiple from the Bates sale. Overall, the $500-thousand invested in buying the agency from Bankers had been parlayed into a $17-million pay-out.

K&B was now part of the largest ad agency network in the world. Since we no longer had to spend our own money, we stepped up plans for international expansion . . . both in Europe and the Far East. In May 1987 the Chicago office moved into a new building on Ontario Street. I had a corner office with a balcony, plus an adjoining office that housed the audiovisual equipment I used to prepare my speeches and seminars.

The Big Turnaround

It seemed like everything was wonderful. Little did I know how things were going to come crashing down for me in the next 12 months.

The changes began in July. The Saatchi management was unhappy. They had paid big bucks for Bates and were not pleased with its performance. So they merged it with another, smaller Saatchi agency. It became Backer Spielvogel Bates (BSB). Jacoby had retired. A guy named Carl Spielvogel was put in charge, with Don Zuckert reporting to him. For some reason, Carl and I never hit it off. Meanwhile, Howard Draft and Zuckert had become close, personal friends.

We were under a lot of pressure to hit our numbers, and we were coming up short. In November, Zuckert presented a reorganization plan that called for putting Howard in charge of our domestic operations, while I concentrated on foreign expansion. That meant I'd be traveling a lot . . . since most foreign trips were week-long affairs. Because of family concerns, it wasn't a good time for me to be gone that much.

Over the next few months, I suggested a couple of viable alternatives. It seemed like Zuckert would agree with them, but Spielvogel would shoot them down. I finally realized it wasn't going to work out. The only other solution I could think of was for me to buy-back the Chicago office. BSB would retain our larger, New York office . . . which would tie-in nicely with their headquarters.

By early 1988, there was a British guy I had been working with, who oversaw all of the Saatchi U.S. agencies. He thought my buy-back plan made sense, and recommended it to the "powers to be" in London. We had not negotiated a final price, but I was prepared to pay $1-million for the Chicago operation.

In mid-March, I had a long-planned trip to Australia. It included some speeches and seminars at the Australian Direct Marketing Association in Sydney, plus a few days of sight-seeing with my wife. I was somewhat reluctant to leave before things were settled, but one of my Saatchi contacts assured me that everything looked good and that the buy-back plan would soon be approved.

We arrived in Sydney on Saturday morning. Early Monday morning, I got a call from Nikki Hanna, a loyal employee, who had worked for me off-and-on since Stone & Adler. With the time difference, it was now early evening in Chicago. She reported that Zuckert had made an unscheduled visit to the office and had spent the day in a series of closed-door meetings with Howard. I called my secretary, Betsy, who agreed that it looked like something funny was going on.

At their insistence, Nikki and Betsy returned to the office that evening to search the wastebaskets in Howard's office. Sure enough, they found copies of memos that showed how things would be run after I was gone. I wasn't sure what was going on. But I knew the Tupperware account now represented about half of the Chicago office billings. It was a well-known Blue Chip account located in Orlando. I reasoned that they probably wanted to switch that account to New York, and let me buy-back the rest of the Chicago office. That didn't seem fair. Especially if they were doing it behind my back.

So I finished my speeches Tuesday, cancelled the vacation part of the trip, and headed back to Chicago on Wednesday. However, instead of going into the office the next day, I booked a secret meeting with Tupperware and headed to Orlando. I disclosed my plans to buy back the Chicago office and asked for their commitment. They were willing to stick with me but felt it was important for me to retain the top creative guy on their account.

On Monday morning, I walked back into the Chicago office . . . as if I had just returned on-schedule from Australia. Howard didn't say anything about the secret Zuckert visit. I met privately with the creative guy Tupperware wanted to retain. Unfortunately, he was someone I couldn't trust. He soon told Howard I had been to see Tupperware.

Meanwhile, I was still waiting for an official answer on my buy-back plan.

It came Friday morning. Zuckert made another unscheduled visit. In a morning meeting, he told me the Saatchi brothers would not approve my buy-back plan. Instead, he had decided it was time for me to leave. Furthermore, if I didn't agree to leave, they would

fire me and void a $500,000 exit payment in my employment con-
tract. I was given until 3 p.m. that day to make a decision.

I had never been in a situation like that before. It was as if I had
a gun at my head. I called our lawyer. He came over and recommended we negotiate a settlement that would allow me to save face.
We reached a verbal agreement Friday afternoon, and reconvened
on Saturday morning to sign a Memo of Understanding. In the matter of a few hours, the agency I had built for ten years was taken
away from me. And it seemed like my protégé had conspired to get
rid of me. That hurt.

As it turned out, I wound up buying my freedom instead of buying the Chicago office. My non-compete agreement was reduced
from two years to one. The agency name was changed to Kobs &
Draft. I would stay around for six months, which gave me the time I
wanted to clean out my files and put together sample notebooks of
our client work.

It also gave me time to think about *what's next.* I could certainly
afford to retire. I had been earning big bonuses and become a mil-
lionaire even before we sold to Bates. I was only 49 years old. I jok-
ingly told people that retiring . . . and spending all day at home . . .
would probably drive my wife nuts and lead to divorce. And if I
wanted a divorce, it would have been a lot cheaper to do it before
the agency sale!

The Memo of Understanding we signed on that "Black Friday"
covered everything we could think of at the time. Some details
weren't mentioned . . . like my accrued vacation pay and my share
of our international bonus pool. Bates refused to pay them. Negotiations dragged-on for a few years. We finally went into arbitration in
June 1992. After a three-day hearing, the judge awarded me

$107,000 in additional compensation. That just about covered my legal fees.

Fond Memories: Being able to reward key staff members with more responsibilities, bonuses, and promotions. One in particular stands out. I had a very attractive secretary, Bobbi Carter, who wanted to be a copywriter. Our creative people thought she was too good-looking to be a good writer. So I had Tom Brady *secretly* give her writing lessons. When Tom said she was ready, Bill Gregory reluctantly agreed to give her a test writing assignment. She really surprised him, got promoted to the creative staff, and went on to become a creative supervisor at another agency.

Lessons Learned: After hearing about my agency exit, you might suspect I learned a lesson about *not* trusting people. That isn't the case. Most of the people I've worked with in business have been loyal and trustworthy.

The main lesson I learned is that you can be *too loyal*. I started working with my lawyer on the employment agreement with Bankers. He was a savvy negotiator and a good legal resource for a small company. But by 1988, we had outgrown him. I'm convinced a stronger lawyer would have provided better advice and got a better settlement when I was asked to leave.

7

Kobs Gregory Passavant
The Second Time Around

A headline in *Advertising Age* on March 6, 1989, announced that "Kobs and Bayer Bess link up." That was almost a full year after the Black Friday when I had agreed to leave Kobs & Brady Advertising. Here's how I decided what to do next.

I started exploring a variety of possibilities while winding things up at K&B. I considered buying a small direct marketing agency and met with some, but nothing clicked. I was contacted by a couple of the largest DM agencies, who offered the opportunity to start a new division or head a Chicago office for them. Flattering, but it didn't excite me. Another possibility I explored was to hook up with a medium-size general ad agency, so they could offer direct marketing capabilities to their clients.

Before long, my last six months at K&B were coming to an end. Yet I still had six months left on my non-compete agreement. So my secretary, Betsy, and I moved into a shared office at 333 W. Wacker Drive—that neat, curved building on the Chicago River. The name of my new firm was the IBJ Consulting Group.

It was a private joke. IBJ stood for In-Between-Jobs. The trade press announced my new affiliation. I thought one of the reporters would ask what IBJ stood for . . . since they obviously weren't my initials . . . but nobody did.

In Fall 1988 things started coming together. The first person who had expressed interest in joining me to "do it again" was Bill Gregory, my former creative chief. He had left K&B a few months after we sold to Bates. I felt we could use a third partner. It struck me that Pierre Passavant might be a good fit. We had worked well together in developing the "Beyond the Basics" seminar, and he had a strong background in consulting. But Pierre was a lifelong East Coast person. I doubted he would want to relocate to Chicago. To my surprise he was very interested as long as I was willing to later let him head a New York office for us.

Of all the agency affiliations I considered, the one that stood out was Bayer Bess Vanderwarker (BBV). They had started as a house agency for Quaker Oats, later becoming independent, but still retaining the Quaker business. I had seen that movie before. It was very much like what I had done with K&B and Bankers. At a lunch meeting with Ron Bess on October 27, 1988, he explained that one of their clients, St. Paul Federal Savings, was pushing them to add direct marketing capabilities. It was like Ted Bates and the Navy on a smaller scale.

The following week I met with Ron's partners: Gary Bayer and Tony Vanderwarker. We all seemed to hit it off pretty well and began to explore an affiliation. I soon decided to *cut to the chase*. I did an agenda for a mid-December meeting that summarized our respective needs and what issues needed to be resolved. They were willing to go along with everything I wanted.

It was time to bring the players together. On December 29, Pierre flew to Chicago for an all-day meeting with Bill and me. I dubbed it the Summit Meeting. I outlined my concept for a DM agency/consultancy and the advantages in affiliating with BBV. Bill and Pierre also went along with everything I wanted, and I sent them each a bottle of champagne to celebrate our emerging partnership.

However, one critical issue had not yet been covered—the equity mix. I wanted the three of us to be equal partners, each owning 25%. The BBV guys would own the remaining 25%. Unlike K&B, I didn't feel it was necessary to be the majority shareholder. But I did need to control my own destiny, which meant I wanted my shares to control the voting rights. There was no way I was going to build another agency and see myself nosed out the door.

I covered this issue individually in follow-up meetings with Bill and Pierre. Fortunately, they understood where I was coming from and went along with it. The BBV guys also consented to my controlling the voting rights.

Summit Meeting II was held on January 28, 1989. We started with a review of the key points that Bill, Pierre, and I had agreed upon. This included the name for our new firm: Kobs Gregory Passavant (KGP). Then we went to meet with our BBV partners and see the office space they planned to sublet to us. It was in Illinois Center on Michigan Avenue. I knew our start-up would be easier if we affiliated with an established agency. They were willing to let us share their phone and payroll systems, office equipment, and insurance program.

We discussed potential clients and prospects. Including our 3 partners, we planned to start KGP with 10 full-time staff members. Finally, we reviewed our initial budget and set April 3 as the target opening date . . . just three days after the expiration of my non-compete agreement.

My concept for the new organization was a full-service agency that also offered *à la carte* creative and consulting services. Most agencies only paid lip-service to consulting. At the time there were just a couple well-regarded DM consulting firms. And nobody had successfully combined advertising and consulting under one roof. I felt we could do it.

Unlike Kobs & Brady, the goal wasn't to grow as big as possible. Or to build and sell. As K&B had gotten bigger, most of my time was spent in winning new business, over-seeing large clients, and the administrative area. This time around I wanted to be meaningfully involved in client marketing and creative projects . . . the more fun areas of the business. To me, that meant we should become medium-size, with no more than 20 to 25 staff members.

We opened the doors with 6 project clients. Our first big account came two months later—a consulting assignment for AT&T's business catalog that later led to creative work. Before the year was up, we added consulting work for MCI. While they were direct competitors with AT&T and clients don't usually let their agencies work for competitors, I managed to convince them we would staff their accounts with different people and take extra measures to ensure confidentiality. We retained both accounts for many years.

A few accounts were referred to us by BBV, though they never

Kobs, Gregory, and Passavant about to launch their new agency.

became a large percentage of our billing. A couple, like Quill Corporation and Mayo Clinic, followed me from K&B. Other important clients over the years were Encyclopaedia Britannica, Field Museum, Nightingale-Conant, Pitney Bowes, and Wells Fargo Bank. We also helped Bose expand their direct marketing business, which lead to a potential conflict.

Bose sold a wide variety of audio speakers through traditional retail channels. Dr. Bose, the founder, felt their Wave Music System should be sold direct to consumers. When they approached us, they had only been successful with radio spots on the Paul Harvey Show. I did monthly consulting trips to Boston, and they were soon getting good results from direct mail and magazine ads . . . with some of the creative work done by KGP. I began recommending television advertising, and brought it up a couple times in meetings with Dr. Bose.

Our client contact phoned me one day to report that Dr. Bose had finally agreed with me. They were ready to test TV. But he hesitated, and I sensed he was uncomfortable about something. It finally came out. They wanted to consider a number of agencies to handle this important assignment—in addition to KGP—but they didn't know *which* agencies they should consider.

Now the ball was in my court. Should I recommend the best agencies, which would be the toughest competition for us? Or suggest some also-rans?

Of course, I did the right thing. And we did not win the TV assignment. But we did win the gratitude of a client that realized he had put me in an awkward position, and I had handled it professionally.

New York, New York . . . That Wonderful Town

In Fall 1991, Pierre moved back East and opened our New York office. We staffed it to handle consulting and account services . . . with creative, media, and production work done in Chicago. The New York office grew steadily for a few years and moved to larger quarters. Unlike K&B, it never surpassed the Chicago office in billings. But it did give Pierre more independence, which he seemed to crave.

When Pierre shifted to New York, we brought in Bob Weinberg as a partner to head the consulting area in Chicago. His background in direct marketing covered a broad range of consulting—from business start-ups to database projects.

I noted that consultants often repeat similar projects for different clients . . . such as the feasibility for a new catalog. I encouraged Bob to develop a predictable model for analyzing the potential success of a new catalog, which could be offered to clients at less cost than a custom analysis. The result was our Catalog Decision Maker. It generated a number of inquiries and accurately predicted the success of one of the most profitable new catalogs launched during that period.

Meanwhile, Bill was suffering from emphysema. He started cutting back on his hours and then retired to California in March 1993. Sadly, he died about a year later. He was a very bright man, who once admitted to me he didn't have the will power to stop smoking. Bill's hand-picked successor was Alan Fonorow, who provided us with great creative leadership for many years.

Our continuity wasn't as solid on the consulting side of the business. Bob Weinberg and I clashed on a few staffing issues. He resigned at the end of 1995. I replaced him with Kevin Leo, who was more an agency guy than a consultant.

The next change came early in 1996, when Bayer Bess Vanderwarker sold their agency. The merger required them to sever our partnership. And it meant we had to find our own office space. We moved to the South Tower in the same Illinois Center building, where my corner office on the 39th floor had great views of Lake Michigan.

The most surprising move of all came at the end of 1996. It was my last day in the office before a holiday vacation in Florida with the family. Pierre phoned, with no warning, to say he was resigning. The official reason was to allow him to pursue a job heading the DM graduate program at New York University. In reality, I think it had more to do with the business prospects for the New York office. Its billings had dropped almost in half during the year, and Pierre had projected an even worse drop for 1997.

I asked him what he thought we should do with the New York office. He said he really hadn't thought about it! That was hard for me to believe. Even though we had worked well together for almost eight years, and he was a partner with his name on the door, it seemed like he was just looking out for himself.

Pierre agreed to stay another month or two. That gave me time, after my vacation, to visit his East Coast clients. We didn't have a likely successor to head the New York office. So we gradually shifted most of the work to Chicago, and closed the office at the end of 1997.

Despite the management changes, KGP had continued to grow steadily our first seven years. Our payroll topped $1 million and we were nearing the maximum size I wanted. Capitalized billings reached $18 million in 1995. Then the problems surfaced with the New York office, and our billings dropped to $10 million annually for a couple of years.

Three Keys to Success: People, People, People

As I had realized early in my agency career, we were really in the people business. We believed in hiring the best people we could find

. . . providing an atmosphere where they could do their best work . . . and rewarding their accomplishments.

We were fortunate to attract many valuable and loyal staff members over the years. One of the best and brightest was Melinda Nykamp, who joined us right after getting her Masters at Northwestern. She had a strong entrepreneurial streak, and I knew it would be tough to hang on to her, but we kept giving her new challenges, and managed to retain her for about five years.

Another key employee was Nikki Hanna, who worked at both K&B and KGP. She capably filled a variety of positions . . . from production assistant to office manager to executive secretary. She was a good judge of people and provided me with an excellent sounding board.

I liked to think of staff members as my business family. However, KGP was also involved with some of my real family members. Karen was working at Nightingale-Conant, when her boss brought us in to help with their catalogs. Our job was to promote the new motivational products that were launched in each monthly edition. A year or two later, Karen was promoted to head the catalog area. It was pretty neat to have a daughter as a client.

Kathy was also a client, briefly, when she worked for Signature. And she was on our staff twice. She originally helped out at KGP for a few months after college. Later, she rejoined us after making her mark at Signature and provided some valuable contributions to accounts like Britannica and Wells Fargo.

In the advertising game, clients make the world go around. Over the years, I worked with all kinds of them from family businesses to giant corporations. Between K&B and KSC, we had about one-third of the top fifty advertisers as clients. And virtually all of them were nice people.

As the years went on, the business seemed to get tougher. There was more competition from new agencies and creative boutiques. Also the Internet was changing the business, and adding more specialists. I decided it was time for me to start thinking about exiting the agency and just doing some consulting. So in 2000 we set up Kobs Strategic Consulting (KSC) as a separate division.

The plan was that Alan Fonorow would acquire the agency part of the business through an earn-out. He liked the opportunity. But before we could make it happen, he had one of those "too good to pass up" job offers from my old agency. Alan took the job.

I was left with a shrinking client list and a reduced staff. By now, Kevin Leo had resigned and been replaced by Brian Paradies. Brian did a good job for a couple years. Before long, we couldn't afford him anymore.

Field Museum was our last remaining client. KGP had originally been hired to double their membership in five years. We actually did it in about three and one-half years. I personally handled the account the last year or two, providing the mailing strategy and supervising the creative work, but outsourcing the media and production. Then I transitioned the account to a team I put together for the client.

It was time to move on. So in January, 2002, Nikki Hanna and I moved to a nearby, shared office with Kobs Strategic Consulting on the door. I did a few consulting projects, joined the board of a printing company, and was quite involved with the Direct Marketing Educational Foundation.

Most of my time was devoted to cleaning out files. Seems like we had always been too busy at year end to go through the year's files and decide what should be saved. It was much easier to just pack everything into transfer files and move them to an off-site storage center. So we did. When the time came to wind down the agency and move KSC, we had over 500 file boxes in storage.

It would have been easy to just have the files destroyed, but I wanted to save a few key documents from each client. Plus the finished samples of our creative work—the ads, mailings, and TV spots we had worked so hard on.

I guess I've always been a saver. I already had samples of almost every ad or mailing I had been involved with throughout my career. The sales letters I had written at Rylander. The creative work I did at Combined and American Peoples Press. Plus the free-lance projects. Then the creative work I did after I joined Stone & Adler. Eventually, I did more account work than creative, but I still managed to save creative samples from all of my S&A clients. And tried to do the same for K&B, and later, for KGP.

I wasn't sure what would eventually happen to all my files and creative samples. Just knew I wanted to save and organize them. Then in February, 2006, I was contacted by Duke University. They wanted to acquire my papers for their advertising and marketing library, which is one of the largest in the U.S.

Hopefully, my files will be preserved. They not only summarize my fifty-year career, they trace the evolution of the direct business. When I started, direct mail and mail order were substantial, but unglamorous—the ugly stepchild of the advertising business, if you will. Today, direct marketing is a vital and dynamic discipline that's used by virtually all major advertisers. It's been great to be a small part of that Cinderella story.

Teddy Bears represented the 3 partners on their Christmas card.

Fond Memories: In the early days of KGP, Kathy took the photos for our Christmas cards. They featured three teddy bears that represented the three partners. Somehow she even managed to get permission one year to shoot pictures of the three bears at Wrigley Field.

Also, having my name tied-in with two major agencies at the same time. Kobs & Draft continued to use that name until 1995, about seven years after I left. I couldn't resist a few smart remarks about the change. So I wrote a brief article for *Advertising Age* entitled: "What do you mean they took my name off the door?"

Lessons Learned: Almost all the clients at Kobs & Brady started with a six-month retainer. KGP was much more project-oriented. So we worked especially hard to do a great job on the first project for a new client. I referred to it as *hitting a home run the first time up.* If you didn't, there might not be a second project. By the way, I learned a long time ago that the same is true when you change jobs in the business world. Get off to a great start the first few weeks, and you'll earn some instant respect from your new boss.

8

DMA
Getting Involved and Giving Back

There are a few activities that were deeply intertwined with my business career—speeches, writing, and my involvement with the direct marketing trade associations. Let's start with the latter.

It began on the local level, with what was then known as the Mail Advertising Club of Chicago (MACC). Their big event and income-producer was Direct Mail Day. Hundreds of people attended a day jam-packed with speeches, seminars, exhibits, and parties. I first got involved in the late 1960s, as a member of the Promotion Committee. I moved up to Promotion Chairman for the 1968 Direct Mail Day and created a series of three mailings to build attendance. Since it was an election year, I used a political theme that positioned Direct Mail as "the people's choice."

The following year I was elected to the Board of Directors for MACC and continued to move up the ladder with Direct Mail Day responsibilities. I was Program Chairman for the 1970 event. My committee lined up all the speakers. For the luncheon, I chose Wally Phillips, who was then the most popular DJ in Chicago. I prepared a nice introduction for him the day before, so I was all set. Or at least I thought I was.

Wally showed up a few minutes before the luncheon. He asked me to "put him down" in my introduction, so he could come back with some humorous insults. So when the luncheon got underway in the Conrad Hilton's grand ballroom, I sat at the head table and rewrote my remarks. I used some lines like "we tried to get the most popular local radio personality—but unfortunately, he wasn't available." The crowd loved it, and Wally was a big hit.

I was General Chairman for the 1971 Direct Mail Day. My 13 committee chairs helped put on a super day, and we drew a then-record crowd of 1,200. At the same time, I served as Vice-President of MACC, and became President in 1972. We had about 500 members at the time. I initiated a number of new activities, including contact with Roosevelt University, that led to establishing the nation's *first* Masters program in direct marketing.

In 1973, MACC changed its name to the Chicago Association of Direct Marketing (CADM). I stayed involved in various roles. On June 20, 1985, I was presented with the Downs Award as the *Direct Marketer of the Year*. My acceptance speech mentioned my dream to play for the Chicago Cubs . . . and how I had built my own team of major leaguers with Kobs & Brady. It was great to have my family there for the presentation, and I fondly remember walking through the exhibit hall lugging my giant trophy.

The following year, the association started an educational foundation and embarked on a major fund-raising campaign. I served as honorary chairman and helped raise over a quarter million dollars. Most of the money went to Northwestern University and was eventually used to fund their Masters program in Integrated Marketing Communications.

Little did I know at the time, that my daughter, Kathy, would later attend the program. Or that, still later, I would spend six years teaching in the program.

My involvement with the national association began in 1966, when it was known as the Direct Mail Advertising Association (DMAA). It later became the Direct Mail Marketing Association and eventually the Direct Marketing Association. I attended my first Annual Conference in New Orleans. I was working at Combined and knew very few people outside of Chicago. It was a great learning experience. There were three days of speeches and seminars, and much helpful info was exchanged. A large exhibit hall also made it easy to see a lot of suppliers in a short amount of time.

Many of the suppliers also had evening cocktail parties. That's where I first met some of the industry leaders I had heard about for years. I met a lot more of them a couple years later, when I started attending the conferences with Bob Stone, who *was* one of the industry leaders.

Things kind of snowballed from there. By the early 1970s, I was serving on committees . . . appearing on conference programs . . . judging awards . . . and handling special projects. I also began bringing Nadine with to the annual conventions, where she attended the spouse programs. We got to visit a dozen U.S. cities, plus Montreal and Toronto. The kids relished us being gone because my folks stayed with and spoiled them.

The field of direct mail and mail order was becoming more

important and beginning to attract big name advertisers. But some-one had coined the term *junk mail*. DMMA responded by forming a public relations committee and hiring a PR firm. Stone & Adler served as the volunteer ad agency. Under my direction, we created ads and mailing inserts to portray the positive advantages of advertising mail. A Mail Preference Service was established. Consumers could write DMMA to have their names removed from mailing lists—or added. Fortunately, most of them chose the latter, making the PR program a ground-breaking success.

We followed that by developing a magazine-style insert for the *New York Times*. My first exposure to the DMMA Board of Directors came when Bob Stone and I presented the concept. The insert was designed to sell the advantages of shopping by mail, and titled "The Store that Never Closes." It appeared in the *Times* on the first Sunday of 1973. The 24-page supplement had articles extolling mail shopping, interspersed with ads from DMMA members.

My involvement continued. Before long I was active in the Marketing Council, organizing programs and panels for conferences, and developing teaching aids for colleges. In 1982, when I was heading Kobs & Brady, I was nominated for my first 3-year term on the association's Board of Directors. I was told it would result in a lot of good friendships. It did. I was told we would get some business from clients that were also on the Board. We did. I was reelected to a second 3-year term, and spent much of it on the Executive Committee, where most of the decisions were made. All in all, it was a very positive experience.

One of my more challenging assignments on the Board was renegotiating a long-standing contract with Pete Hoke, the publisher of *Direct Marketing* magazine. The original agreement provided that all DMMA members would receive an annual subscription to his publication, which was very costly to the association. Previous attempts to renegotiate by various board members went nowhere. Pete was a friend of mine. So I volunteered to negotiate with him under one condition—that he and I could still be friends afterwards. Pete agreed to this.

We met almost once a month for the next year. They were tough meetings. I'd try to get one point agreed to at each session. Usually Pete wanted to back-track at the next meeting. But I persevered. After four file folders full of notes, we signed off on a one-page statement of intent and turned the details over to the lawyers. The agreement we reached was fair to both parties. And Pete and I remained friends. In 2001, I helped get him elected to the DMA Hall of Fame.

My own election to the Hall of Fame was in 1999. I first learned about it in June of that year, while on a family vacation in Colorado Springs. We celebrated with a fancy dinner and a bottle of 1995 Opus One. Another celebration took place that October in Toronto, when I was formally inducted. The DMA showed a nice video history of my accomplishments.

Reaching Out to Students and Teachers

Back in 1966, DMAA leaders recognized the difficulty of attracting advertising students to a career that was best known for doing direct mail. It formed a separate, but affiliated organization: the DMA Educational Foundation. It, too, had a series of name changes over the years . . . until it became the Direct Marketing Educational Foundation (DMEF).

My involvement with DMEF started when I worked for Bob

Stone, who was one of the charter board members. There was always a board meeting at DMMA's Spring Conference, which Bob never attended. So I got to attend the Foundation's meetings for him.

Late in 1980 . . . in the early days of Kobs & Brady . . . DMMA President, Bob DeLay, asked if we would create a *pro bono* brochure for DMEF. I turned him down. I felt the Foundation needed more than a new brochure. I felt it needed a marketing plan to expand and maximize its potential, and I was willing to donate our efforts to create the plan. Bob readily agreed.

The plan was presented at the Foundation's board meeting in March 1981. It spelled out five objectives, with appropriate strategies and tactics for each. One key recommendation was to focus activity on teaching the teachers, as a more cost-effective way to get our message to students. The plan was very well-received and guided the Foundation's direction for many years to come.

In 1990, I was able to attend meetings of the Direct Marketing Educational Foundation on my own. I was elected to the Board of Trustees and served a six-year term. By 1998, the Foundation had grown substantially, and a new Strategic Plan was developed. Even though I was no longer on the Board, I was asked to work with the committee and help present the plan. It was approved.

Two years later, when the nominating committee was developing its slate of candidates, I was called upon by President Dick Montesi to rejoin the Board. Dick had been effectively leading the Foundation since 1980. Like Bob DeLay, he had become a good friend and was hard to turn down. This time I got even more involved and served on the Executive Committee.

The association had always been supported by a combination of annual donations and special one-time gifts. For example, in 1989, I had contributed $50,000 to fund research done by the academic community.

By 2001, the Foundation had a new president, and we were having trouble getting contributions. The trustees voted to turn the Ed Mayer Award Dinner into a fundraiser. That meant substantially boosting the ticket price and adding some silent auction items before the dinner. The event was slated for Chicago, as a kickoff to the DMA annual conference. I was asked to chair the Dinner Committee. We sold tables and individual tickets. The dinner was a smashing success—we had over 300 attendees and raised $103,000!

The dinner continued to grow in prestige and profits the next few years. We expanded the auction to include some live items, which were offered after the dinner. When we ran out of attractive items to bid on one year, I had our auctioneer ask for scholarship donations. Two years later, the annual awards dinner raised over $250,000, including $100,000 in scholarship contributions, and the Foundation's financial health was greatly improved.

Meanwhile, I was elected to a two-year term as DMEF Chairman in 2002. I had some great board members and committee chairs. Together, we reversed the Foundation's financial problems . . . developed a new Strategic Plan and mission statement . . . and expanded our educational programs.

All told, I think I spent fourteen years as a DMEF trustee. Plus my earlier involvement with CADM and DMA. It was, of course, a way to give back. As I said when I was elected to the DMA Hall of Fame, the direct marketing field has been very good to me. I'm glad I had the opportunity to serve with so many fine people, and hopefully, my efforts have made a difference.

Croquet players join Bob DeLay (left) at a DMA Board reunion.

It's now been 28 years since I joined the DMA board, but the friendships continue. Bob DeLay started a reunion group, which takes fun trips every year or two . . . highlighted by a formal croquet match. In 2006, I started writing a newsletter for the retired members of the DMA board, which gives me a good excuse to stay in touch with those who helped shape and lead the association.

Fond Memories: Before attending my first DMA convention, I had heard New Orleans was known for its many fine restaurants. The first night I had dinner at Galatoire's in the French Quarter, which was excellent. I had no dinner plans for the next night, until a supplier invited me to join his group. I eagerly accepted, only to find out later we were going to Galatoire's. So my only two opportunities to sample the city's great cuisine were at the same restaurant.

Also, DMEF's award dinners were always held in October, during the DMA annual convention. That meant there were important baseball games going on — the play-offs or World Series. I started a tradition by bringing along a radio headset so I could keep other baseball fans posted on the scores.

Lessons Learned: When I was president of CADM, a state legislator introduced a bill to restrict the rental of mailing lists. He was known as someone who introduced meaningless legislation, which he would withdraw if he got a substantial contribution from those who would be negatively affected. We held a special meeting of influential club members to discuss alternatives. The majority felt we should just pay him off rather than fight the legislation. I went along with the majority, but I've always regretted it. A leader should be out in front leading his group to do the right thing, not following the majority.

9

Speeches and Writing
Sharing Words of Wisdom

When I took that first speech class in junior college, with my knees knocking behind the podium, who would have guessed I'd go on to deliver over 285 business speeches and teach more than 75 seminars?

It started when I worked at Stone & Adler. Bob Stone got a lot of speech invitations and accepted most of them. Sometimes he'd invite me to join him. One talk I developed for us contrasted creativity in some classic old-time ads with their more modern counterparts.

If Bob had a conflict or wasn't interested in doing a talk, he'd suggest I might be interested. I was happy to get his rejects. Doing speeches and writing articles helps build your reputation. It's also good exposure, especially if you're in the agency business. Occasionally, you even get a new business lead or a client from someone who was in the audience.

An early talk I fondly remember was at a DMEF Collegiate Institute in June, 1969. The week-long institute was lead by Ed Mayer, who had an all-star line-up of guest speakers. One of them was Bob Stone. Don't remember why, but Bob asked me to fill in for him. I was nervous. Not just because Ed was famous and I was a young kid. But because he had a reputation as a tough critic and would tell you exactly what was on his mind.

So I carefully chose a case history of a direct mail test program I had just developed for one of my clients—the Airline Passengers Association. I presented it with lots of slides and flip charts. Then I held my breath. When I was done, Ed said it was one of the best test programs he'd ever seen!

That fall was another key talk. The Mail Ad Club of Chicago usually had out-of-town speakers for their monthly luncheons. The one slated for September had to bow out. I was asked to substitute. One of the neat things about direct marketing is being able to scientifically split-test different variables to see what works best. Does one creative approach improve response over another? Do you get more orders when you offer a free gift? I developed a talk that showed what we had tested for various clients, and with their permission, shared the results. It was well-received, and I did updated versions of that talk for a number of years—including one at a DMA conference with over 400 in the audience.

When I started doing speeches, I would write out the whole talk. Later, I'd work from an outline . . . but I'd still write out the beginning and end. So if I got nervous or lost my place, I knew I could start out strong and finish smoothly. This was before computers and

PowerPoint, so I usually relied on slides for illustrations. As you can imagine, preparing a new talk takes considerable time. Thus, I really appreciated the opportunity to repeat a speech, with just minor updating, rather than develop a new one.

Some of my favorite repeats were "10 Steps to Long-Range Direct Marketing Success," "The Multi-Media Marriage," and "Proven Direct Response Offers." I learned a valuable lesson when I was doing my Offer talk at a University of Wisconsin seminar. I was given more time than normal. Instead of just doing my usual lecture, I got the audience involved in analyzing offers and brainstorming improvements. And guess what? They not only learned the subject matter better, their speaker evaluations were higher than in the past.

Most of my talks were at DMA conferences, Direct Marketing Days, or local ad clubs. The clubs would usually invite a guest speaker for their lunch or dinner meetings. In those situations, I felt the best formula was to mix humor with a serious message. My first big success with this formula was in April 1978. My book had just been published, and I was doing a luncheon talk in Houston. The first half of my remarks described the humorous experiences in becoming an author, such as the one-sided standard author's contract, which gives the publisher the rights to virtually any future use of your material you can think of . . . including comic books and Broadway plays.

I then segued into the serious part of the talk, which covered some of the book's case studies. When I checked my records, I found I did this speech at least 17 times in the 1970s and 1980s. Later, I developed an Agency President talk, which followed the same formula. After describing the lighter side of the agency business, I high-lighted some important industry trends.

Another talk I did from Coast to Coast was on marketing strategies. It was adapted from my DMA seminar, and was the first thorough explanation of how to strategically approach a direct marketing program. The talk was featured as a cover story in the May 1987 issue of *Direct Marketing* magazine and was also offered on cassette to the publication's subscribers.

The most prestigious direct marketing event back then was the International Direct Marketing Symposium. The week-long affair was held each spring in Lausanne, Switzerland, and attracted about 2,500 attendees. I was asked to present there for the first time in May 1981. It was quite a production. Speeches were presented on 4 giant, side-by-side screens and simultaneously translated into English, French, and German. You had to submit your talk in advance, so the text slides could be made for each language.

My three-hour time slot called for me to discuss what is now called B2B or Business Direct Marketing. I titled the talk: "How to Reduce Selling Costs and Increase Profits." It included success stories ranging from Hewlett-Packard to Xerox. My presentation was quite well received, and I was asked back a couple times.

The symposium was run by a rather tight-fisted German, Walter Schmid. He would pay a nominal amount for your travel expenses, but would not reimburse the cost of making your slides or pay an honorarium. However, he always devoted one evening to a special Speakers Dinner. It was an elegant affair, held in a cave on the outskirts of town. The food was great, and the spirits flowed all night.

The symposium was promoted with an extensive 32-page brochure. About a month before my 1981 talk, I was contacted by an

Marketing Strategies featured as a magazine cover story in 1987.

IBM executive. He was planning an international advertising meeting in Milan the week after my scheduled appearance in Lausanne. Would I present the same talk at their event?

Of course, I accepted. It was a nice train ride from Geneva to Milan. I happened to have a former employee living it Italy, who graciously played tour guide for me on the weekend. I reciprocated by introducing her to an Italian agency executive I had met at the symposium, who hired her at a much higher salary because she had been trained at Kobs & Brady in the States.

So my first two international talks were delivered only a week apart. Over the years I made presentations in ten different countries. They included Australia . . . Canada . . . France . . . Norway . . . South Africa . . . the United Kingdom . . . and finally, in China. But none of the others treated the speakers to dinner in a cave.

Teaching Seminars

The first seminars I taught were in Fall 1977. *Advertising Age* was doing a series of one-day seminars that were like a week-long roadshow. Other speakers covered subjects ranging from public relations to sales promotion. I was recommended to teach direct marketing.

Week one had all the seminars taught in New York, with week two in Chicago, the following week in Denver, and the last week on the West Coast. I developed a one-day overview of direct marketing basics. It was successfully repeated in 1978. Later on, I often taught an updated version of that seminar at Chicago Direct Marketing Day and similar venues.

At the same time, DMA was offering a popular three-day seminar taught by Pierre Passavant. Many attendees wanted to go on to something more advanced. DMA had nothing to offer, and Pierre didn't want to do all the work to prepare a new seminar on his own.

Dick Montesi was then heading DMA's education department. In 1983, he approached me about partnering with Pierre to develop an advanced seminar. After a couple of meetings, we were ready to go ahead—if we were reasonably sure it would be successful. Neither of us wanted to do the prep work and find there wasn't enough interest to continue. So we did a research mailing to DMA members. The results: there was definitely an interest. Also, they preferred a fifty/fifty mix of lecture and case study.

From having Honeywell as a client, I had learned quite a bit about security systems. I suggested we develop a fictional case study of a firm that sold a portable home security system via mail order. We dubbed the company P&K Electronics (for Passavant & Kobs). For each seminar subject, such as media or creative, Pierre or I would lecture on the subject. Then we'd get the attendees involved in applying these principles to P&K. For example, *here are some ads created by P&K's ad agency. What's good or bad about them? Do they follow the creative principles we discussed?*

There was a concern that if we made the seminar too advanced, it would limit the market. So we positioned it more at an intermediate level, and called it *Beyond the Basics*. We did a test run with K&B employees, then taught the first two-day seminar for DMA members in November, 1984.

Wish I could say it was an instant success. It wasn't. It took a couple years to refine and polish the presentations. Attendees filled-out a detailed evaluation form after each session, which rated various aspects of the content, presentation, and speakers. With an average audience of 40 to 45, it's difficult to please everyone. And comments can be quite critical. As an example, I was once criticized for wearing a *brown* suit . . . even though it was brand new and I was wearing it for the first time!

While all the evaluations and comments were carefully reviewed, I always felt there was one key question. Namely, would you recommend the seminar to others? We averaged a 94% approval rate on this important question.

After a couple of years, Pierre decided to stop teaching. So I continued the seminar on my own until April, 2001. DMA would normally offer the seminar to its members 3 to 4 times a year, mostly in New York and Chicago. But we also drew well in areas like Colorado Springs and San Diego. In resort areas, I would adjust the second day schedule to finish in mid-afternoon. We'd normally do an informal cocktail party the first night or I'd buy a round of drinks in the hotel bar.

Larger firms could arrange with DMA for a private seminar on their own premises. I did over a dozen privates over the years, including three for AT&T. On average, I taught the seminar more than four times a year, and had over fifteen hundred total attendees. Of course, the seminars had to be squeezed into my normal working schedule. But the promotion mailings kept my name out there. And at least a couple seminar attendees turned into good clients—including Shopsmith and Bose.

The material was updated and new slides added regularly, with a few major revises along the way. A typical seminar included about 270 slides, some TV spots, and a half-dozen involvement exercises. Eventually I added a whole segment on the Internet. One thing that didn't change much was the P&K case study. When we first developed it, there weren't any portable security systems on the market.

A 1986 seminar promotion mailing.

As we went along, Black & Decker started making a product almost identical to the one I'd invented for P&K. I used to kid that Pierre and I should have gone into the security business instead of the seminar business.

From Seminars to Semesters

Looking back, it seems like a natural evolution. If you can teach a two-day seminar, why not a semester-length course? In Spring 1986, I agreed to teach an undergrad course, one evening a week, at Northwestern University's downtown campus. Naturally, I used my book as a text. The syllabus adapted some of the material from my DMA seminar.

Knowing my travel schedule would make it tough for me to attend every class, I chose one of my colleagues, Sid Liebenson, as co-instructor. We repeated the course together in Spring 1987.

One thing I liked about the course was a longer opportunity to work with the students. With my seminar, I felt I was just getting to know the students by the end of the second day. Then they were gone. By comparison, the course stretched-out for 14 weeks. I enjoyed teaching, and taking the students out for pizza and beer after the final exam.

Following a few year hiatus, I began teaching a graduate course for Northwestern in Fall, 1993. This one was offered two mornings a week at the Evanston campus. I was still traveling a lot, so I again recruited one of my staff members to co-teach. Bob Weinberg did it the first three years, and Kevin Leo the next three.

Teaching graduate students was a challenge. They were more likely to question direct marketing practices . . . even if things had always been done a certain way. In other words, they kept you on your toes. Some of them stayed in touch after graduation. It was rewarding to see how they matured and the great jobs they got with well-known corporations.

My last teaching assignment was for the University of Chicago. I was on a committee to help them plan a Direct Marketing certificate program. They eventually settled on a five-course program, and I agreed to teach the opening three-day course. This was in October 2003. Unfortunately, my course was the only one that had a decent number of attendees. So after teaching it a couple times, the program was "temporarily put on hold." In academia, as is often the case in the business world, it meant the end of the program. But how many people have the privilege of teaching for both Northwestern and the University of Chicago?

As mentioned earlier, seminar evaluations can be quite critical. But if you do a good job, you also get a lot of nice feedback. A number of my Northwestern students commented that I really seemed to *care* that they understood the concepts being presented.

After presenting my Marketing Strategies talk at an international meeting in Europe, one of the attendees came up afterwards and told me she couldn't wait to get back to the States. She thought she had developed a sound marketing plan for her business . . . but now felt it had to be totally revised to follow the marketing strategies I'd outlined.

One of the nicest compliments I ever received was from Bob DeLay. After one of my DMA talks, he wrote: "You have a rare talent, Jim, and it is marvelous that you are willing to share it with our audiences."

Written Words

Writing has always come easy for me. Over the years I had a number of articles published in the trade press. Topics included creativity . . . offers . . . selecting an ad agency . . . and direct marketing careers. *Advertising Age* even published a couple of humorous pieces I did.

As noted earlier, I worked with Bob Stone when he wrote his direct marketing best-seller in 1975. It was so successful that the publisher wanted him to do a follow-up book, consisting largely of case histories. Bob declined. But he suggested I might be interested in writing such a book. Actually, I was . . . and I wasn't.

My job was pretty hectic at the time, plus the usual family demands on the home front. I did want to write a book some day. Was this really the right time to do it? In the end, I decided "a publisher in the hand is worth two in the bush." In other words, I could write a book anytime . . . but might have trouble finding somebody to publish it. In this case, I already had an interested publisher. And not just any publisher. This was the book division of *Ad Age*, which meant my book would get promoted in their publication.

So I agreed to do an outline and write a sample chapter, which was quickly approved. The outline covered three sections: How to Start a Direct Marketing Program; Improving a Successful Direct Marketing Program; and Case Studies. I suggested a dozen chapter-length cases that would cover the direct marketing spectrum.

About half of them were current or former clients, like Hewlett-Packard and Sunset House. These wouldn't require much research, because I already had files and samples from working with them. The rest would be more difficult. I'd have to research the firm . . . gather sample ads and mailings . . . decide the story angle I'd build the case around . . . and get permission to share some proprietary info. I was afraid the latter would be a tough challenge. The solution was to conclude each chapter with a brief *Insider's Viewpoint*, written by one of the firm's executives.

That gave me the perfect opening to contact the potential companies. I told them I was writing a book and planned to include a detailed case study about their firm. And by the way, would you be so kind as to provide some insider comments, which will appear over your name and title? This was classic misdirection. Get them to think about seeing their name and comments in print . . . rather than think about the info I needed and would share with the world.

The strategy worked. With only a couple of exceptions, I got the cooperation I wanted. I also did my homework. I bought a few shares of stock in the public companies, so I could get their annual reports. I researched relevant articles that had appeared in print. I listened to cassette recordings of speeches by company execs at industry events. So I was even able to include case studies of firms like Fingerhut and Haband, who had always been reluctant to share much about their marketing and promotion.

Finding the time to write was a struggle. By the time I got home from the office, had dinner, and spent a little time with the family, it would probably be at least eight o'clock. Get the book stuff out. Remember where you left off. Start writing. Before you know it, the 10 p.m. news is on and you're getting a bit tired.

One solution that helped me get in extra writing time was to stay up one night a week, usually on Monday, until 3:30 in the morning. Fortunately, I could do that and still function well the next day. I also spent some week-end and vacation time pounding my typewriter. In August 1976 we did a vacation at a rented cottage near

Lake Geneva. Nadine would take the kids to the beach during the day, while I typed away at a card table. The cottage wasn't air conditioned, so I often stripped down to the waist. But 4 chapters got written those two weeks.

By the time I got done researching, writing, editing, and proofing the book, I had spent a grand total of 1,032 and one-half hours. That comes out to about 26 forty-hour weeks, or a half-year of normal work time.

On July 29, 1977, I delivered the completed manuscript to my editor, Mel Brisk. He said: "Now you're an author." Of course, you're not really an author until the book is published. I'm still not sure why, but Mel sat on my manuscript for almost a year. That turned out to be a tremendous break. The book was finished during my last full year working for Bob Stone. If it had been published promptly, it would have identified me as working for Stone & Adler.

Instead, I didn't hear the publisher was moving ahead with the book until the following May. I was then the new President of Kobs & Brady Advertising. I finished the requested revisions that fall. A year later, in October 1979, the first copies came off the press. It was titled *Profitable Direct Marketing*—and positioned as "how to start, improve, or expand any direct marketing operation . . . plus detailed case studies of prominent direct marketing companies."

At the time, there was some confusion about semantics. So the book added my own definition: *Direct marketing gets your ad message direct to the consumer to produce some type of immediate action.* Thus, it includes direct mail, catalogs, print ads with coupons, telemarketing, and TV with 800 numbers.

As I said in the Preface: "Writing this book has been a tremendous experience. It brought back fond memories of client programs I was involved with. It gave me new insights into some specialized areas. And it helped me put in perspective a lot of things that make direct marketing such an exciting and fast-growing area."

The book was great exposure for my young ad agency. *Advertising Age* kicked-off the promotion with a double-spread ad and bind-in order card. I did a trade-off with the publisher. We donated the creative work for their ads and mailings in exchange for copies of my book. Copies went to clients, staff members, and new business prospects.

The book sold quite well and was reprinted a number of times during the next 10 years. A business book club ordered 2,000 copies. Foreign translations were published in Portugal and Indonesia. But the case studies eventually became dated. The publisher wanted me to write a second edition. We exchanged correspondence off and on for a couple years. In April 1986, I submitted a detailed outline for how the new edition would be expanded and what changes were required.

I chose to delete the chapter-length case studies and just intersperse mini cases throughout the text. The outline called for 22 chapters, 12 of which were new. We decided to retain the original title, even though over half the material was not in the first edition.

It was harder to get into it the second time around. Probably because this time I knew how much time and effort goes into writing a book. I made little or no progress the next few years. Perhaps because I had a few other things on my mind, including winding up my affairs at Kobs & Draft. Plus deciding what to do next, and getting another new business off the ground.

The publisher eventually suggested I find a freelance editor to help me with the 2nd edition. Sort of like a ghost writer. I agreed to give it a try, and was introduced to a woman named Anne Basye. Luckily, we hit it off well.

On the chapters that were repeated from the first edition, I would mark up the chapter and give Anne detailed notes on what I wanted to change or add. Most of the new chapters were based on material I had developed for my seminar. So Anne would get a copy of my seminar notes plus pages of handwritten notes on how to adapt the material. Then she would write the first draft. I would edit it. And she'd make the final revisions. As I later noted in the book's introduction: "This edition is much better than the first one because of her dedication."

I started working on the second edition in September 1989 . . . about six months after starting my second agency, Kobs Gregory Passavant. It took just over a year to get the book done.

By now, *Ad Age* had sold their book division to NTC, and I was working with a new editor. When my first edition appeared in 1979, there were only a handful of books devoted to direct marketing. By 1991, there were already over 200 books on the subject. Yet when my editor got done reading the final chapter, she called and told me: "This is the best direct marketing book yet written."

We kicked off the book's promotion with a speech at the DMA's annual conference in Boston. The goal was to have the first copies there, so attendees could buy an autographed copy. Unfortunately, they didn't arrive in time. However, I did finally get to autograph copies at a Barnes & Noble bookstore in suburban Chicago. And just to show how famous I had become from all my speeches, seminars, and articles, I think a total of five people showed-up! And one of them was a relative!

Fond Memories: Teaching a seminar in a New Orleans hotel, when the fire alarm went off. I thought we should evacuate, but the attendees didn't. So we kept going. Thank goodness, it was a false alarm.

Also, there are a lot of details involved to make sure a seminar comes off smoothly. The DMA would usually ship your material in advance, including the attendee notebooks. Normally, you would arrive at the hotel the night before your seminar started and make sure everything was on hand. One 1999 seminar in San Antonio was a rare disaster. The material I found in my meeting room was for a funeral directors seminar! And the first day was half-over before the hotel could track down and deliver the right material.

Lessons Learned: One is pretty obvious—be prepared. That means knowing what you're going to cover in a speech or seminar, as well as checking out all the audio/visual equipment to make sure it is working properly. Less obvious is a lesson I learned early in my seminar days. It's okay to give attendees a list of topics you'll cover. But *don't* give them a schedule of which topics will be covered at what time. You often get behind schedule. Some attendees get nervous if they know you're running late. But it's pretty easy for an experienced teacher to catch-up and finish on time. So there's no need to worry anyone.

10

CELEBRITIES
Getting to Know You

Between Nadine and me, we have partied with Frank Sinatra . . . dined with Gregory Peck . . . had a private lunch with Mayor Richard M. Daley . . . attended a wedding for Paul Harvey's son . . . sang with Sandi Patti . . . had a picture taken with Henry Kissinger . . . enjoyed cocktails with super model Claudia Schiffer . . . received an award presented to me by Bob Newhart . . . square danced with President Jimmy Carter . . . and met Prince Rainier at the Royal Palace in Monaco.

In the sports world, I was visited at La Rabida by Joe Garagiola

. . . got batting lessons from Ron Santo . . . played softball with Randy Hundley . . . and golfed with Hall-of-Famer Fergie Jenkins.

The business world gave me a chance to know Senator Robert Kennedy's son, Christopher, who ran the Merchandise Mart . . . the audio expert, Dr. Bose . . . the co-founders of Hewlett-Packard . . . and the heads of numerous successful direct marketing businesses.

I won't bore you with all those encounters. But I do want to share our memorable trips with the Sinatras and the Carters.

It was Fall, 1989, when a Chicago newspaper columnist ran a brief item about an upcoming charity event that began at the Sinatra home in Palm Springs and wound-up in Las Vegas. I called the paper and got a contact number for the event. Another call brought the invitation. As a long-time Sinatra fan, this sounded too good to pass up . . . a chance to attend a "Magic Carpet Week-end" and meet Frank.

Nadine wasn't sure she wanted to go. But I talked her into it. On Friday, November 17, 1989, we boarded a morning flight to Palm Springs. The event was starting with a 3:30 cocktail party at the Sinatra residence. It was a fundraiser for the Barbara Sinatra Children's Center.

The hosts had arranged for a limo to meet us at the airport and take us around town until the event started. We've always wanted to make sure our charitable contributions were worthwhile, so we opted to visit the Center, which aids abused children. We were impressed with the facility and its programs, especially some of the things they were doing to restore the kids' self-esteem.

Our next stop was at 70-588 Frank Sinatra Drive. Per our instructions, we arrived about an hour early, so we'd have time to change and freshen up. We were assigned to one of the guest houses around the pool. I got ready a little before Nadine, and began looking around. Across the hall, in the same guest house, was an artist's studio. The door was open, and the room was empty, so I went in. The easel had a half-finished painting.

It was one of many that were spread around the room. All the finished canvasses were signed *Sinatra.* I had been a fan for over thirty years, and I never knew Frank was a painter! I got to see a private showing of his paintings, which were all contemporary or abstract.

A few minutes later we strolled over to the big house for the cocktail party, and were greeted at the door by Barbara Sinatra. She was a former Las Vegas showgirl, who had previously been married to Harpo Marx, and was still very attractive. She quickly made sure we got a drink, introduced us to another couple who were guests, and whisked us over to meet her husband.

The invitation had mentioned there would be Sinatra friends and other celebrities at the event. However, it didn't mention any names. So we weren't sure if we'd really see anyone we'd recognize. The only familiar face I spotted on the way in was Tom Dreesen, the comedian who often opened for Sinatra.

Barbara introduced us to Frank and then disappeared to greet other guests. We were suddenly standing alone with him, and he didn't seem too happy to be there with a bunch of strangers at his wife's charity event. What do you say to break the ice? I tried: "I see Tom Dreesen is here. Is he going with us tonight to Las Vegas?" Frank coldly replied: "Of course, he's going with us. He's one of my guys."

I wasn't sure what to say after that. Fortunately, I didn't have to worry about it, because other folks were being brought over to meet

Frank. We joined the couple who Barbara had graciously introduced us to and began people watching. They weren't kidding about celebrities. Before the cocktail party was over, we spotted Dick Van Patten . . . and then Gregory Peck. Both with their spouses.

An hour later, we were shown to a group of waiting white limousines and driven to the Palm Springs airport. Besides the celebrities, there were 38 guests in the group . . . plus two Sinatra secretaries and Jilly Rizzo, Frank's friend and bodyguard. We all boarded a private jet for the half-hour flight to Vegas.

Another group of limos met us at the Las Vegas airport and took us to Bally's Casino Resort. We never saw the lobby. We were given our room keys as we left the plane and brought to a private entrance of the resort. An elevator took us to our pre-assigned suite, where our luggage was soon delivered. It was a well-appointed suite with living room, bedroom, bath, and bar. Not a mini bar. This bar was stocked with full bottles of premium booze.

There was just time to unpack and have a quick drink before the next cocktail party. This one was at 8:00 p.m. in a private meeting room at Bally's. A few other celebrities joined the group, including Shirley Jones and Rich Little. Nadine and I were chatting with Frankie Avalon and his wife, when Barbara came over. She said to me: "Frank's sitting at the bar alone. Why don't you go talk to him?"

After the cold reception at his house, I wasn't so sure I wanted to talk to Mr. Sinatra anymore. But I was ready for a refill. So I strolled over to the bar, ordered my drink, and decided I'd make one more effort to start a conversation.

I mentioned that our guest house was next to his studio, and I was impressed with his paintings. "How long have you been painting?" I asked. The question was a great ice-breaker. He told me it started many years ago, when he was a band vocalist with Tommy Dorsey. They were appearing at the Paramount in New York City. It was common in those days for leading entertainers to perform in big-city movie theatres. They might do four or five brief stage shows a day interspersed with a feature film.

Frank said he got bored between shows, and one day he dropped-in at a nearby art museum. It was pretty empty. Then a teen-age girl and her mother walked in. As the girl spotted him, he could hear them whispering. She said: "That's Frank Sinatra!" The mother replied: "What's he doing here?"

The next day he went to an art supply store and told them he wanted to buy everything he needed to become an artist. He continued painting over the years, but now he did it mainly at home in the pre-dawn hours. When he performed, he was used to being up half the night. At home, he'd often wake at 3 or 4 in the morning, and be unable to go back to sleep.

So he'd head to his studio and paint. Before long, some daylight would be peeking through the windows and their gardener would show up. He would be the first one to admire Frank's artistic endeavors.

Once I got him loosened up, it was easy to keep the conversation flowing. I asked him about his son and daughters. He talked enthusiastically about them, like any proud parent would. Before long, it was time for dinner. I rejoined Nadine and we headed to an adjoining room. We found our name tags at one of the round tables, and waited to see who would be seated by us.

Our dinner partners included Tom Dreesen, plus Gregory Peck and his wife. Nadine, who I had to talk into taking the trip, was now having dinner next to a handsome and famous movie star. She asked him about his children and his latest film. I couldn't hear much of their conversation because I was too busy talking to his wife, Veronique. She was a former French journalist, who had been sent to interview Greg when he was in Paris. They had been married for many years.

After dinner, we topped off the evening by seeing Bally's big variety show from upfront tables. Saturday was a little less hectic. There was an informal luncheon and fashion show for the ladies. The afternoon was free, so Nadine and I played tennis.

The evening started with another private cocktail party. Then we all attended a roast for Tommy Lasorda, the long-time manager of the Dodgers. Still more celebs showed up for the roast, including sports figures Steve Garvey and Harry Caray. Knowing the roast was on the agenda, I had stuck a baseball in my suitcase, which I got autographed by Frank and Tommy.

Things wound up with a Champagne Brunch on Sunday. Then we headed back to Chicago. The trip had cost $25,000. But the money went for a good cause. The weekend was all I expected—and more! I figured it would be tough to top a trip like this. We did, three years later.

Joining the Sinatras in Monaco

After the Magic Carpet Weekend, we were invited every year to the annual Sinatra celebrity golf outing. It sounded nice, but wasn't a high priority.

Then, in Spring 1992, we got a special invitation. The Sinatra's were chairing a week-end in Monaco with the Royal Family to celebrate the tenth anniversary of the Princess Grace Foundation. I thought it sounded pretty neat. Nadine felt we'd be surrounded by the rich and famous . . . people with whom we had nothing in common. (Turned out she was right.) Somehow, I still managed to talk her into going.

The invitation not only outlined three packed days of events, it suggested the proper attire for each. Women get more uptight about things like this than men. So a lot of fretting and shopping went into preparing Nadine's wardrobe. She bought and borrowed and finally packed a big suitcase of finery.

We started with a few days in and around Geneva, Switzerland. I wanted to show Nadine where I had attended the International Direct Marketing Symposiums. And it gave us some time to get over the jet lag before arriving in Monaco on a warm and muggy Friday in August. We checked into the Loews hotel. Our welcoming package said a chartered bus would be in front to take us to the evening's reception. It was at the Royal Palace.

A few hours later, the bus let us off at the Palace gates. And we strolled through a receiving line that included Prince Rainier . . . Princess Caroline . . . Prince Albert . . . Barbara Sinatra . . . and Frank Sinatra. Waiters were waiting with trays of drinks for the cocktail hour. Then there was a private concert in the courtyard. We enjoyed the Royal Orchestra playing Mendelssohn, Tchaikovsky, and Greig.

Then it was back on the bus for a trip to the harbor. We boarded a stunning yacht for another cocktail party and buffet supper. The yacht was owned by John Kluge, who made a fortune in the media business. He had sold his Metromedia business in 1984 for $4.65 billion! We later found his yacht had taken three years to complete and was considered among the finest ever built. One of the crew told me it was nicer than the one owned by Prince Onassis.

Other celebrities on hand included superspy Roger Moore, plus Gregory Peck and his wife. The celebs seemed to stick together more than they had at the Las Vegas event, but there were plenty of other high rollers around. They included Leo Jaffe, the retired chairman of Sony Pictures . . . John Johnson, owner of Ebony Magazine . . . Prince Ali Khan . . . and Alfred Heineken, whose beer is well known.

Saturday morning, our bus was waiting outside the hotel. The word had gotten out about the celebrities who were part of our group. So a small crowd was gathered around the bus to gawk and take pictures.

Before long, we were doing our own gawking. Our luncheon was at the legendary villa La Fiorentina in Cap-Ferrat. This estate was owned by Mr. and Mrs. Lawrence Harding. A rather famous couple. He had headed Braniff Airlines. She was better known as Mary Wells and had won his advertising account before winning his heart. Their retirement home was high above the Mediterranean and surrounded on three sides by water.

We strolled outside to enjoy the view, the gardens, and a string quartet that was playing on one of the patios. Prince Albert said hello, and we chatted briefly with him about sports, before being seated for lunch. Our table included his sister, Princess Caroline.

We discussed her interest in ballet and horses . . . her children . . . and the foundation. We learned it supported the arts in the States and the needy in Europe. Our table also included Robert Tisch. He had introduced himself as the head of the Princess Grace Foundation. I assumed it was his full-time job. In an awkward *faux pas*, I asked him what he had done before joining the foundation. He said: "the same thing I'm doing now . . . I'm the head of Loews Corporation." No wonder we were staying in a Loews hotel.

Meanwhile, Nadine was checking out the wardrobes of the other women. One of them was completely clad in Chanel, from her suit and bag to her shoes. My wife's wardrobe was considerably less expensive, but she looked lovely in a linen and lace dress, topped with a white hat. She also wore a rhinestone pin. One of the ladies complimented her on it, and was surprised to learn it was a gift from my mom. The woman thought Nadine had a very generous mother-in-law, because in this crowd, they just assumed she was wearing diamonds, not costume jewelry.

My own wardrobe was more modest. But I did wear an ascot to the luncheon, which I felt gave me a rather sporty look.

It was soon time to do another wardrobe change for the big Saturday night event, the Red Cross Gala. As usual, the evening started with a cocktail party. I returned from the bar to find Nadine and another lady chatting with a very attractive young woman. They felt sorry for her because she seemed to be alone. Her name was Claudia . . . she was from Germany . . . and told us she had recently started doing some modeling. We later learned she was Prince Albert's date, and Claudia Schiffer went on to become a rather famous model.

The Red Cross Gala was considered the big event of the Monaco season. Our group was joined by a who's who of the social set. Frank Sinatra was the entertainer, and did a great concert. We ate, drank, and danced the night away with some of the world's most beautiful people.

The next day we were on our own. It was time to visit the casino and do some sight-seeing before heading home. We strolled around Monaco . . . had a bite to eat . . . and browsed in shops. By late afternoon, we were exhausted and ready to head back to our hotel. But we couldn't find a taxi and didn't have the local coins to phone one.

We finally managed to catch a bus. It was amazing how our fortunes had changed overnight. We had descended from the private celebrity bus to where we belonged, with the commoners!

From Royalty to the Presidency

As a long-time Republican, I'm pretty sure I never voted for Jimmy Carter. But I had discovered his Carter Foundation and made some nominal donations to it over the years. Then early in 2008, I read President Carter's book, *Beyond the White House*. It's the story of his post-presidency and traces what the foundation has accomplished in its first twenty-five years. I was very impressed by the scope of their activities, from waging peace to fighting disease.

The first chapter explained how the Foundation had grown and become financially sound. It also mentioned that some major contributors are invited to an annual meeting in Atlanta. President Carter and Rosalynn get to thank their supporters, and the supporters get an update on the foundation's programs. It had been 16 years since our last celebrity trip. Maybe it was time for another one.

A phone call determined that those who contributed $1,000 or more were eligible to attend the annual meeting, plus an optional day trip to visit the President's hometown. There were only a few spots left, so I quickly sent a check.

We flew to Atlanta on Wednesday, April 24, 2008. Our contact at the Carter Center, Susie Hubbard, had invited us to dinner that night . . . where we met her boss and a few other attendees. Thursday morning was free, so we got together with one of Nadine's high school friends and strolled to a nearby park.

The Carter Center Executive Briefing, as it was called, began in the afternoon, with the showing of a recent documentary film about President Carter. That was followed by a cocktail reception and a very nice dinner. The evening program was on "Battling Disease at the Grassroots Level in Ethiopa." A panel discussed the shortage of health care workers and how the Carter Center was training a skilled national workforce.

Day two started early, with an 8:00 a.m. continental breakfast. The morning included a two-part briefing. One showed some of the major diseases that are common throughout Africa. Such as Guinea Worm, a two-foot-long parasite that grows inside the body and finally pops out, causing excruciating pain. The Carter Center's two-decade battle is close to eradicating this disease . . . which will be the first ailment to be totally eliminated since smallpox in 1977.

Other diseases being fought include Trachoma, the leading cause of preventable blindness . . . Malaria . . . Elephantiasis . . . and River Blindness. Most come from parasites in the ground water that is used for everything from bathing to drinking. Water filters, donated drugs, and millions of insecticide-treated bed nets are used to prevent and control these devastating diseases.

The session also touched on mental health, which has been Mrs. Carter's favorite cause since she was the First Lady. She has written a couple of books on the subject. Thanks in part to the Carter Center's lobbying efforts, legislation was finally passed in 2009 to prevent discrimination against those who suffer from mental illness. It requires health insurers to provide benefits that are comparable to those for physical illnesses.

The other morning briefing covered the Carter Center's peace programs. Their efforts monitor elections in places as diverse as Nicaragua and the Democratic Republic of the Congo. They distribute democracy information in Beijing and promote avenues for political reform in China. They have also negotiated some important international peace agreements.

After another nice lunch, we awaited an afternoon session with Jimmy and Rosalynn Carter. They had just returned from a trip to the Mid East, which included meetings in Israel, as well as discussions with Hamas leaders.

The Carters presented an overview of their trip. Then someone commented that President Carter had been involved in Mid East peace negotiations for over a quarter century . . . dating back to when he was President.

He told us a fascinating story about the Camp David Summit Meeting in September 1978. He had brought together Menachem Begin from Israel and Anwar Sadat from Egypt. They began a week-long series of meetings. President Carter said that they weren't making much progress, because the two men were constantly battling So President Carter decided to separate them, and act as go-between. He went back and forth between their two cabins and said he put in some long hours. Rosalynn interjected that one session lasted all night and it was 6 a.m. before he returned. On the last full day of negotiations, the principals conceded the peace agreement would not get done. They were still too far apart on some key issues. A press conference was scheduled for the next day to announce the sad news.

In a last-ditch effort to salvage the agreement, the President got copies of a photo taken when the summit meeting started. It showed Sadat, Carter, and Begin smiling, in anticipation of a successful meeting. He then found out the names of Menahem Begin's grandchildren, and autographed a picture for each of them.

Jim and Nadine Kobs with Rosalynn and Jimmy Carter

Next, he took the photos to Begin's cabin and said: "I thought you might like to give these to your grandchildren to show that you at least tried to negotiate peace with Egypt. Menachem Begin began to cry and said: "That's not the legacy I want to leave my grandchildren. We'll get it done tomorrow." And they did. The President's last-ditch strategy saved the day!

The Friday events concluded with a Presidential reception. But first, each couple had their picture taken with President and Mrs. Carter. There was only time for one take, so we had to hope it turned out well. (Fortunately, it did . . . and we received an autographed copy a few weeks later.

When the picture-taking was over, the Carters mingled with the guests on the grounds of the Carter Center. Besides munching and drinking, there was time to browse through the Carter Presidential Library & Museum, which is connected to the Center. It contains interesting exhibits, including a replica of his White House office and pictures of Plains, his home town.

It was a nice preview for our Saturday bus trip to Plains in Southern Georgia. It's about a three-hour ride. Plains is still a small town, with one main street and a population of about 650 people. We were welcomed at Plains High School, which is now a museum. President Carter told us about growing-up there . . . leaving to become a Naval officer . . . and returning to stay when his father died. He and Rosalynn also answered a few questions. Then lunch was served at the Plains Community Center.

The afternoon started with a three-mile train ride to the Jimmy Carter boyhood home. His family grew peanuts. Their farm had a modest home, with a nearby barn. Our guided tour of the property included some small cabins, where the black farm workers lived, and a one-room country store.

We would spend Saturday night at a local motel in a neighboring town. But first, we did a self-guided tour of Plain's Main Street. It is only two-blocks long, with a couple of stores selling souvenirs and peanuts. We also got to see the Presidential Campaign Headquarters in the old train depot. A Southern barbecue was slated for 5:00 p.m., with square dancing to follow.

Shortly before dinner, the Carters joined the group. Mister Jimmy, as he is called by his neighbors, was wearing blue jeans with a denim shirt and a red bandana. Rosalynn wore a white sweater with casual slacks and shoes. They mingled with the crowd, then got in line with the rest of us, and filled their plates for dinner. We were seated at a picnic table near the one the Carters had joined. It wasn't as fancy as a Presidential dinner at the White House, but it was good.

After eating, it took a while to clear the tables and get ready for the square dance. The Carters were walking around. Nadine got to ask Rosalynn about their family, while I chatted with Mister Jimmy about baseball.

I knew he was an Atlanta Braves fan, so I asked if his busy travel schedule allowed him to get to many games. He said only a couple a year, but he did watch as many games as he could on TV. I reminded him that the Braves should be thankful the Cubs let Greg Maddux get away. The President said he had gotten to know Greg and thought he was a fine young man.

Before long, Main Street was set up for dancing. There were three musicians with guitar, fiddle, and banjo . . . plus a square dance caller. We started by forming squares of eight dancers. Then we'd circle around and do-si-do with our group. We were not in the same group with the Carters. But after a bit, you parade your partner in a big circle, and all the men move-up to join a new partner. Before long, Nadine had the President as her partner, while I was dancing with Rosalynn. For a few moments, Nadine and Jim were dancing with the stars.

After a long number, we were glad to take a break and catch our breath. Mister Jimmy was then 83 years old. Yet, he and Rosalynn danced every number. When they finally retired, he said he had to finish preparing his Sunday School lesson for the next morning.

We had been told it was customary for the President to teach whenever he was at home in Plains. Moreover, it was a popular tourist attraction with first-come, first-serve seating. That meant boarding our bus at 6:30 a.m. Sunday morning. A short time later we were watching the sunrise at the Marantha Baptist Church and waiting for the doors to open.

When they did open, we had to go through a security check by the President's Secret Service detail. There was even a bomb-sniffing dog on duty. The church was packed, but we were early enough to get a good seat upfront. The President arrived a bit later, and picture-taking was allowed until he started his lesson. This wasn't a Sunday School lesson for the kids. He stood upfront, where he could talk to the whole church.

His hour-long lesson was followed by the regular Sunday Service. After that, they had box lunches ready for our tour group, which we enjoyed on the bus ride to the Atlanta airport. I took quite a few pictures on the trip. The last one was at the airport, with Nadine on the phone. She couldn't wait to tell our kids about this once-in-a-lifetime trip.

As it turned-out, it wasn't just once. We did the Carter Center trip again two years later, in 2010. It was nice, but there was no way it could top the first one!

Fond Memories: Getting to know the Sinatra secretaries definitely had some advantages. When "my buddy" Frank was doing a concert in Chicago, I would usually try to get tickets on my own. But if I didn't get good seats, I'd appeal for help. Frank's secretary once got us seats in the second row at the United Center, across from Irv Kupcinet, then Chicago's most popular newspaper columnist.

When Sinatra was performing at Poplar Creek in September

1990, I got advance approval for us to go backstage and say hello. At intermission, we went to the backstage entrance. After checking with a couple of different security people, we were cleared to head to Frank's dressing room. There Barbara greeted us and got us drinks. Frank was busy chatting with local celebrities, including the Chicago Bears owner, but we did get to greet him . . . before returning to our seats to enjoy his performance.

Lessons Learned: Celebrities might be famous, but if you get a chance to talk to them one-on-one, they respond to the same things as ordinary folks. They'd much rather chat about their interests than yours. Come to think of it, that pretty much holds true for everyone I know.

11

Sports
Watching, Managing, & Playing

I'm glad to have grown-up and lived most of my life in Chicago. It's not only a world-class city, it's a terrific sports town. A town with some great sports heroes. Like Ernie Banks, Michael Jordan, and Walter Payton. I've been fortunate to see them all play, both in person and on TV.

I've also been able to attend some memorable sporting events: the Bears victory in the 1985 NFC Championship Game; Northwestern losing the 1997 Citrus Bowl to Tennessee and Peyton Manning; the Kentucky Derby in 2002; and the 2010 marathon tennis match at Wimbledon.

The first Super Bowl I went to was XVII in 1983. I took Ken to see Washington beat Miami at the Rose Bowl in Pasadena. We were seated in the next to the last row. He returned the favor by taking me to see the Cardinals and Pittsburgh in 2009, but we had much better seats. In between, I saw Super Bowl XXX in Arizona. So I guess I'm on an every-13-years Super Bowl schedule.

When it comes to baseball, I've seen even more memorable games: They include a couple of All-Star games, plus:

- The "Sandberg" game in June, 1984 . . . when Ryne hit two game-tying homers.
- Pete Rose getting hits number 4,190 and 4,191 on September 8, 1985, to tie Ty Cobb for the all-time most hits.
- The long-awaited first night game at Wrigley on 8/8/88 . . . which eventually turned into a rain-out.
- And the Arizona Diamondbacks very first game on March 31, 1998.

But there's no contest: The best game I've ever seen was Game 7 of the 2001 World Series. Yankees at the Diamondbacks. Ken somehow got us seats in the very first row behind home plate. We saw great pitching . . . Roger Clemens vs. Curt Schilling . . . with no runs until the D-backs scored in the bottom of the 6th. But the Yanks tied it in the 7th and went up 2 to 1 in the 8th, bringing Randy Johnson on in relief. The Yanks countered with their great reliever, Mariano Rivera, who struck-out two in the 8th.

As the bottom of the 9th started, I remarked what a great game it had been—even if it looked like the D-Backs were going to lose. But then Mark Grace led off with a single. Five batters and one out later . . . the crowd was on its feet as Luis Gonzalez blooped a game-winning hit over short. The Diamondbacks thus became the quickest expansion team to win a World Series. What a game!

The pros usually put on a good show. But as any parent can tell you, there's nothing like watching your own offspring perform. In my case, that includes Karen at gymnastics . . . Kathy at soccer . . . and Ken at football and baseball.

Our 8 grandsons have also been involved in a wide variety of sports that range from basketball to lacrosse. We've seen a number of them make game-winning plays and be chosen as all-stars.

For example, we watched Ken's son, Nicholas, almost single-handedly win his 2007 league championship game. He pitched in relief in the last inning and struck out the side with the leading run in scoring position. He then drove in the winning run in the bottom of the inning. More recently, Karen's son, Michael, made the game-winning kick in his football play-off game.

Managing: The Good News Bears

My managing career began in 1976, when Ken started Little League. He was eight years old. Our team was the Colfax Bears. We had a winning record the first half of the season, when the kids batted off a tee. The hitting was better than the fielding, so it was not unusual to have a score of 34 to 19 or 47 to 25. Then we switched to live pitching. The other teams apparently adjusted to it better than we did. We lost six straight, including the play-off game.

The Colfax Bears returned the next year and had a better season. We won our first six games and finished the regular season 10 and 2. Ken had a great year. He played shortstop and first base and wound up with a .760 batting average. We came from behind in the play-offs and briefly took the lead. But we lost a one-run game on a walk-off homer.

After two years of managing, I decided to take a break and let

Ken play for other managers. It's tough managing your son, even if he's a good player. You try not to show favoritism. Yet you know some parents are sitting there and wondering why their kid doesn't bat clean-up or play every inning.

Maybe that's why you tend to be tougher on your son than on the others. I still remember tossing Ken out of a game. The ump called him out on strikes, and he muttered a swear word or threw his batting helmet as he walked away from the plate. I didn't wait to see what the ump would do. I just told him he was done for the day. Fortunately, it was near the end of the game—so even though I tossed one of our best players—we hung-on for a one-run victory. But I'm still not sure if I would have done the same with another kid.

My last hurrah as a manager came in 1980. By now Ken was 12 and about to play his second year in the majors. I talked a good friend, Steve Berman, into co-managing with me. Unfortunately, we inherited a last-place team. And we started out playing like one. We lost five of our first seven games. But then we got it together and reeled-off five straight wins.

A 13 to 12 victory in our last game allowed us to squeak into the play-offs. That meant we got to play the first place team—a team that had lost only one game all season. We played them tough, but lost 7 to 3. So I retired as a manager with a lot of fun memories, but without ever winning a play-off game.

Playing Tennis and Softball

I started playing tennis with friends in 1954, when we were at Schurz. I played occasionally with friends in college but didn't pick up a racket again until the mid-seventies, when we lived in Palatine. Little did I realize I'd still be playing over thirty-five years later.

My main tennis "partner" since 1977 has been Max Downham. We started playing on Monday nights because we both were traveling a lot, but usually were in town at the start of the week. Max was a better athlete and tennis player than I was. But I was determined to improve. So I started recording our weekly scores on 3 x 5 index cards, along with a few notes. It took about seven years before I finally won a season series.

Then in the mid-eighties, Max started doing more international trips, which meant he was usually gone all week. So we started playing about 7:30 on Sunday mornings instead of Monday nights. That worked-out better for Max than me. He had grown up on a farm and was used to getting up with the roosters.

By comparison, I am not a morning person. So Max started winning more than his normal share of games. I'm too competitive to just let that happen. So for many years, instead of going to bed on Saturday night, I would purposely fall asleep in my recliner chair and set an alarm for 5:00 a.m. That gave me a chance to have a couple cups of coffee before we played and make things more even.

Unfortunately, we don't get to play weekly any more. Max eventually moved to a downtown condo, and we winter in Arizona. But when we're both in town, he drives all the way to the suburbs for our Sunday morning battles. And they're still as competitive as ever . . . with a lot of running and long rallies.

Over the years, Max and I have gone to a couple of out-of-town tennis camps together, and played regularly at a number of suburban clubs. While we belonged to the Meadows Club, I joined their singles league . . . and somehow managed to win the championship in 1996 and 1998.

Thanks to good speed and anticipation, I manage to get to most shots and keep the ball in play. One of my favorite compliments was: "you're like a human backboard. You return everything." Also, I usually win a lot of points with my lobs.

While I still enjoy singles, most players my age only play doubles. In Arizona, I've been playing doubles with Jerry Quigley's group since 1996. They are almost all older than me, so the tennis isn't that competitive, but the guys are fun. I go out of my way to praise my partner for a good shot or a good try. Building them up seems to make them play a little better when they're my partner.

Back home in Chicagoland, I play doubles a couple of times a week with a group that my friend, Dick Honquest, introduced me to. It's called the Donut Gang, since they started on Sunday mornings and take turns bringing donuts. These guys are more my age or younger and are very competitive. I've always felt it improves your game to play against better players. So if my game has improved any the last few years, I have the Donut Gang to thank.

Softball is another sport I still enjoy playing. Originally it was a once-a-year thing at family picnics. When we moved to Palatine, our homeowners group played in a league against other subdivisions. Even though our average age was quite a bit older, we had some good players and won the championship in 1978 and 1979. I was a late-inning sub with limited playing time, but I did bat over .400 one year.

After not playing for about fifteen years, I joined Palatine's senior softball league in 1994. We usually have 14 guys on a team. If everyone shows up, we'll have 11 on the field and 3 guys on the bench. I'm usually one of the bench warmers. But everyone gets to bat, and I play the field four or five innings . . . preferably at second base or catching. Overall, I'm a better fielder than a hitter, and I've still got good speed on the bases.

My best game was in August, 1997. The guy who regularly played short center didn't show up. I took his place. It seemed like almost every ball all night was hit in my direction. And I handled them all cleanly. I caught a line drive . . . a pop-up . . . made force outs at second . . . and started a couple of double plays. We won the game, and I was given the game ball. That doesn't seem so unusual, except I've been playing in this league for 17 years, and it's the <u>only</u> time I've seen anyone be awarded a game ball.

Looking back on the years I've played tennis and softball, I know I've never been a great athlete. But I've always been very competitive, and like to think I've made the most of my limited talents. Especially considering I've only got one good eye, which limits my depth perception. I'm glad I can still participate in sports at my age.

After watching a grandson's game in Arizona a few years back, it made me think that baseball is a metaphor for life. Kids are like first base. They play catch with their dads . . . backyard baseball with their friends . . . and join a Little League team.

As they get older, they move to second base. The fortunate few get to play on travel teams and in high school or college.

By the time they get to third base, their baseball careers are usually over. So they switch to a spectator role and cheer for their favorite team. If that team happens to be the Cubs, they get known as long-suffering fans . . . spend a lot of time waiting for next year . . . and hope the Cubs will get to the World Series before they get to home plate.

Fond Memories: My Father's Day gift from Ken in 1992 was a trip to the Field of Dreams. I still remember the August day when we arrived at the Iowa field where the movie was filmed. As we got out of the car, Ken noticed some people on the diamond . . . and thought there was a game going on that would prevent us from playing. But it so happened they were other baseball fans just like us.

So after walking around and into the corn fields, we got our gloves and took the field. We moved from one position to another as players drifted in and out of the game. And before long, we got our turns to hit. Ken had brought along one of his favorite bats. When it finally came time to leave, we noticed that somebody had cracked it. And we agreed there's no better place for a bat to end its career than on the Field of Dreams.

Lessons Learned: If you're playing a team sport, and you're not one of the best athletes, you can still have fun. And be a valuable team member. I like to think I'm the best cheerleader on my softball team. I make it a point to learn everyone's name, even the new players. And I cheer for them by name on every play they make. Everyone likes recognition, including yours truly.

12

Cubs
Still Chasing a Dream

We had this big console radio in the living room on Halsted Street. It was October 1945. I rushed home from school to listen to the end of that afternoon's World Series game. The Cubs had won the National League pennant—and my favorite player, Phil Cavarretta, was the MVP. Now they were battling Detroit, and looking for their first Series win since 1908.

I vaguely remember listening to the final outs as the Cubs lost the seventh and deciding game of that Series. Do I really remember that? Or was it just a dream? Little did I know it would be the first of many disappointing dreams. But I haven't given up . . . the Cubs are still my favorite team.

The first game I remember attending was with Aunt Frieda. It was a Ladies Day, when women got in for 25 cents. We were seated in the first row down the right field line, near the bullpen. I was keeping score. Somebody hit a sharp line drive in our direction. I had my glove and wanted to try and catch it. My aunt was afraid I'd get hurt, so she tried to cover me up, and the man next to me caught it. He was so impressed that a little eight-year-old kid was keeping score that he gave me the ball.

Over the years I've been to enough Cubs games to catch a few foul balls. Besides attending games at Wrigley Field, I often planned our family vacations with the Cubs schedule in mind. So I've seen them play in St. Louis, Milwaukee, Atlanta, Denver, and a few other cities.

Thanks to the Cubs, we've been enjoying Arizona for more than thirty years. Back then, the DMA would have a Spring Conference in March . . . usually somewhere on the West Coast. We'd stop in Phoenix for a few days after the meeting to see a couple of Spring Training games. We fell in love with the area, began to stay longer, and eventually bought our Scottsdale home in 1993.

Once I had my own agency, I could easily take off work for opening day. I attended the Cubs home opener for the first time in 1981. Two years later, we bought a weekend season ticket package and had two box seats down the right field line. I wanted to get better seats the following year. So I told my secretary to find out the renewal deadline and get to know someone in the ticket office, whom she could contact to get first crack at a pair of good seats.

She did, and reported that the Cubs had some very good seats, behind an exit in Section 126, row 5. But her contact said there were 4 seats and they didn't want to split them up. I asked to see a map of the stadium. The location looked good. And you still didn't have to take the seats for every game, just for weekends.

We really lucked out. Some people say we have the best seats in all of Wrigley Field. The first year in our new seats, we saw the Cubs win their division and get to the play-offs for the first time in 39 years. They beat the Padres in the first two games, both at Wrigley and were one win away from the World Series. Then they lost three straight games in San Diego.

But things weren't all bad in 1984. Ken was on an All-Star team coached by former Cubs catcher, Randy Hundley. One fall day I got a call at the office from Randy. He asked if I was Ken's dad. He said he was looking for help to promote his fantasy baseball camp, and happened to spot my book at a local bookstore. Would I be able to help him promote his camps? I tried not to show how excited I was, and we arranged a dinner to discuss it.

When we got together, I quickly realized his camps were a pretty small business. At the time, Kobs & Brady was handling a lot of big, national clients, and our minimum retainer was $15,000. I tried to tactfully explain that Randy might not be able to afford us.

He quickly got the point and suggested a trade-off. We'd do some advertising for him and I could attend the Cubs Fantasy Camp. That was right up my alley! I've always believed in being loyal to clients and using their products. Here was a chance to play ball with some of my Cubs heroes at their Spring Training home in Mesa. Where do I sign up?

My First Fantasy Camp

I suspected this would be a once-in-a-lifetime experience. Not wanting to forget any of it, I decided to take along a mini tape recorder. Each night, while they were fresh in mind, I dictated my notes on the day's events. They eventually became a 9-page document titled an *Adman's Baseball Diary*. Following are some of the highlights:

Sunday, January 20, 1985—The big day finally arrives. We leave from Chicago, where the temperature was a record-breaking 27 degrees below zero last night . . . and head toward Phoenix, where it's reported to be a balmy 70-degrees. Almost a 100-degree difference!

On the plane, I go through my file on Randy Hundley's Adult Baseball Camps. It has info on what to bring along and important instructions, such as "make sure your toenails are clipped short enough to prevent rubbing or irritation."

At the opening reception, Randy introduces the former Cubs players. They include Ferguson Jenkins, Glenn Beckert, Ron Santo, and Hoyt Wilhelm . . . with Ernie Banks scheduled to show-up a few days later. Randy explains ballplayers are expected to do a lot of drinking, and anyone found in their room <u>before</u> 1:00 a.m. will be fined.

Monday—Walking into the locker room is a real thrill. Over each person's locker is their name and uniform number . . . with their official Cubs jersey hanging in front. My number 44 was the same one Phil Cavarretta had worn.

After some instructions, we're divided into six teams. We rotate among different instruction areas: the batting cage . . . working on rundown plays...catching fly balls . . . practicing baseball situations . . . more batting practice . . . and fielding grounders. Four hours later, we leave the field. The trainer's room is a popular place after the work-out.

Tuesday—This afternoon we play our first intra-squad game. I'm on Ron Santo's team. After striking out the first time, I hit a clean single and drive in a run. I'm batting .500 and wonder if I should quit while I'm ahead. We win 8 to 7.

After the game, I feel pretty good except for some minor problems. Such as a bone bruise on my catching hand . . . a little soreness in my legs . . . and some "jock itch" in my crotch. I walk to the local drug store to buy some remedies, including my first tube of Ben-Gay.

Wednesday—I wake up feeling like somebody walked all over my body during the night. But the game must go on.

I come up to bat with a man on first base. As I step into the box, I glance down to 3rd at coach Santo, and notice he's flashing a sign. Let's see, we only had two signs to remember: one for bunt and the other for a hit-and-run. I assume he wants a hit-and-run, so I swing away and hit a double down the right field line. When I get to second base, Santo calls time, and comes over to ask me how come I missed the bunt sign. He mildly chews me out, then shakes my hand for getting a good hit.

After the game, I join other players in the hotel's whirlpool. The warmth is wonderful, but the outside temperature is a bit chilly . . . and I soon feel like I'm coming down with a cold.

Thursday—The first time up, I hit a clean single. I am also safe on an error . . . score two runs . . . and ground-out twice. We win a close game 9 to 8.

That night I turn in early to try and get rid of my cold. By now, the bathroom counter in my hotel room looks like a miniature drug store, with everything from suntan lotion to cold remedies.

Friday—After having our group picture taken, we play our last intra-squad game.

We lose this one, but wind-up in second place with a 3 and 1 record. I managed to get one hit a day for a .333 batting average.

Earlier in the week, I was moved from right to center field. I play a flawless center field. Well, actually, a catchable fly ball has not been hit to me in the last three days. But I'm very confident. I know I could have caught one if only it had come my way.

Saturday—The rookies are scheduled to play the 1969 Cubs this afternoon at HoHoKam Stadium, the same park where the real Cubs play their Spring training games. I'm nervous and wake-up a couple times during the night. I finally get up and cut my toenails again.

Before the game, each player is introduced individually. We run out and stand along the foul line, just like at a World Series game. The big game goes by too quickly. The '69 Cubs win 11- 7, but we give them a good battle. I only get up once. Fergie Jenkins, a future Hall-of-Famer, is pitching. I slap a hard grounder to short and am thrown out.

At the banquet that evening, the Cubs players take turns presenting a number of awards and trophies. Ron Santo starts talking about a player he could always count on. Someone who continued to get better as the week went on. "And the award for the most improved player in camp goes to Jim Kobs." What a way to end a wonderful week. Can't wait to get home and tell the family about this.

I stay in touch with one of my rookie teammates, Clar Krusinski. In 1989 he puts together a deal to buy the Peoria Chiefs . . . the Cubs Class A affiliate . . . and is looking for investors. I put in $25,000 and suddenly I'm a minority owner of a minor league baseball team. It's a good opportunity to learn more about the business side of baseball. We sold the team five years later for a nice profit.

Back to the Play-Offs

After 1984, it took five more years for the Cubs to get back to the play-offs. In 1989 they won their division by six games and faced the San Francisco Giants in a best-of-seven series. Both Mark Grace of the Cubs and Will Clark of the Giants were hitting everything in sight. And the Giants soon had a two games-to-one lead.

Having regretted not going to San Diego to see one of the final 1984 games, we contacted Sheila Martin, a business friend from San Francisco. She graciously agreed to share her seats for game five. We boarded a flight on October 8 and were in the air during game four. The Cubs needed a win to even the series. They didn't do it. But we were ready for game five at Candlestick Park.

Or we thought we were. Having heard for years about the cold winds coming off the bay, we brought heavy clothes for football weather. But the temperature was unseasonably warm, and we had to scrounge around in the hotel gift shop for some leftover summer wear. Unfortunately, the Cubs' bats weren't hot enough. It was a good, close game, but the Giants scored the go-ahead runs in the bottom of the eighth inning and won 3-to-2.

The next wait was even longer. Sammy Sosa was leading the 1998 Cubs, and he finished with 66 homers. It looked they were going to barely miss the play-offs, but thanks to a last-minute win by Colorado, they wound-up in a first-place tie with the Giants. That meant a one-game tie-breaker at Wrigley. This time the Cubs prevailed. But the enthusiasm was short-lived. They lost in the first round of the play-offs to Atlanta.

Maybe the Cubs would do better in the next century. They started 2003 with a new manager and modest expectations. We took Kevin and Ryan to a doubleheader on the last Saturday of the season. The Cubs won them both to clinch their division title. The fans were celebrating wildly after the game. As we crossed Clark Street, Nadine was interviewed by a TV reporter. We got home in time to see her on the 10 p.m. news. Would the Cubs get knocked out again in the first round of the play-offs?

Not this time! They won the series with Atlanta. Next up—the Florida Marlins. The Cubs would be heading to Florida the same time we were. I was registered for the DMA convention in Orlando. We headed South and watched the Cubs win game 4 at the home of our good friends, Joan & Tom Hanus. That put the Cubs up 3 games to 1. They lost the next day. No problem. They were heading back to Wrigley with their best two pitchers lined-up to start game 6, and if necessary, game 7.

It didn't look like it would be necessary, but it was. They were cruising along with a lead in game 6. Then a fan interfered with what looked to be a catchable foul ball. An error by the shortstop followed, and things fell apart rapidly. They had been only five outs away from the World Series, but the Marlins won game 6, and clinched the series the next night.

Hey, we're not giving up yet. The Cubbies got back to the play-offs in 2007. But they lost three straight play-off games to Arizona. Let's try again in 2008. This time we meet the Dodgers in the first round of the play-offs. They couldn't lose three straight again, could they? They could—and did.

Fantasy Camp:
Better the Second Time Around

When I finished my first Fantasy Camp, I didn't expect to do it again. But I had said a great experience would be even better if you could do it with a friend or family member. I guess Ken remembered that. He surprised me with the camp as a special gift for my sixty-fifth birthday. This time it would be he and I going.

We waited a year so we wouldn't be gone when Kathy's son,

A rookie at the 2005 Cubs Fantasy Camp.

Christopher, was born. It was January 23, 1985, when we attended the camp's opening party. Ken had a great week, and wound-up leading our team with a .615 batting average. I held my own and finish with a respectable .280 average. But we somehow manage to lose all ten of our intra-squad games. That means we'd be the last team to play an inning against the former Cubs in the big game on Saturday.

Randy Hundley has now been doing these fantasy camps for 23 years. And the ex-pros have never lost to the rookie campers. We take the field for the final inning with a slim lead. Our team adds two insurance runs, and we shut-down the Cubs in the bottom half for an upset victory. The Cubs players can't believe it. They come to the banquet that night with pillowcases over their heads.

As I write this, it's the first month of the 2010 season. It's now been 65 years since the Cubs have appeared in a World Series, and 102 years since they've won the Series. They've been playing games at Wrigley Field since 1914, without ever hosting a World Series champion.

I bought a commemorative brick that's outside Wrigley Field. It says: "Waiting for the next World Series. The Kobs family." I'm getting up in years. Sure hope we don't have to wait much longer!

Fond Memories: I have a lot of good Cubs memories. But my favorites are playing ball with my son at the Fantasy Camp. When he was in centerfield and I was at second, we teamed-up for a rare 8 to 4 force-out. We also batted back-to-back. And in one of the intra-squad games, we scored our team's only two runs.

Lessons Learned: I knew our oldest grandson, Kevin, was upset when the Cubs didn't quite make it to the World Series in 2003. I wrote him a letter afterwards that pointed out some reasons why baseball is my favorite sport: "I enjoy watching my grandsons' games, as well as playing softball. When you're out on the field, you quickly learn it's not as easy as it looks. Sometimes you get a big hit. Sometimes you strike out. The same is true for the professional ballplayers that are our heroes. When things don't turn-out the way you want in baseball—or in other areas of our lives—you just have to try to stay positive and do better next time." As I told Kevin, I look forward to taking him to a World Series *one of these years!*

13

Success Secrets
What Worked for Me

It's tough to define success. Some people think of it in terms of the money or the possessions they acquire. For others, it's how many rungs you climb on the corporate ladder. Still others would cite intangibles . . . like earning respect or sharing happiness with those you care about.

Equally debatable is how successful my life has been. As you've seen from the wrap-ups of the previous chapters, I've learned a lot of lessons along the way. I've also discovered a number of tips and techniques that worked for me. They have certainly made my life easier and more rewarding. Maybe some of them will help you become more successful.

Other People's Knowledge. You may have heard of Other People's Money or OPM. I prefer OPK. Ever since my college years, I've been a big reader of books, magazines, and newspapers. Not just a passive reader. But someone who marks important sentences, tears out articles, makes notes about things I want to remember. Some get filed. Others just get piled-up.

Many have been saved longer than they should have been. But all were things I thought were important. Things I could learn from others and, hopefully, recall when I needed them.

Positive Thinking. I was a positive thinker before I ever went to work for W. Clement Stone, but he certainly reinforced the concept with his publications. Success Unlimited magazine included a monthly column by Norman Vincent Peale, the best-selling author of *The Power of Positive Thinking.*

The more self-help books I read, the more strongly I believed that *you are what you think you are.* The mind is a magical thing. If you think of yourself as smart and successful, you tend to become that way.

Unfortunately, it also works in reverse. Negative thoughts lead to negative results. When I'm around people making negative remarks, I usually try to deflect their thoughts and give them a positive spin. For example, let's say we're on the way home from a party. Someone in the car says something negative about what a friend said. I might comment that maybe they didn't mean it that way. Of course, I don't really know if they meant it or not. I do know, though, that a positive attitude makes good things happen.

Your Greatest Power. That was the name of a classic self-help book we sold at Combined. It was a small volume written by J. Martin Kohe. The concept was simple: the greatest power a person has is *the power to choose.*

Think about it. Your life is brimming with choices. Tonight you can choose to watch a so-so TV program or read a good book. You can come home from work tomorrow for a pleasant dinner with your family or spend the dinner hour complaining about the traffic. You can choose to continue in the same career or choose to get trained for something better. The choice is yours.

Never Expect What You Don't Inspect. Motivational authors use a lot of catchy phrases to get their points across. This one, from W. Clement Stone, really helped me in my business career. It suggests you need to follow up to make sure you get what you want.

Let's say I've assigned an important creative project for a new client. The creative team agrees they'll have it ready next Wednesday so I can present it to the client at a Thursday meeting. I get busy with other things and don't check on it until Wednesday morning. Only to find there were some problems and it won't be ready for 2 more days. That could leave me with an unhappy client.

On the other hand, suppose I had checked on Monday to see if my project was going to be ready on schedule. I learn some other projects have delayed its start. However, it could still be ready by Wednesday if I insist. Because I inspected, I can get what I expect and need to meet my client commitment.

Do More than You Are Paid for. If you want to get ahead when you're working for others, it takes extra effort. In the advertising business, our formal hours were 9 to 5. But it was not unusual to work until 6:00 or 7:00 p.m. I always worked at least one night a week at the office and a lot of Saturdays.

When I was the boss, I felt I had to set a good example. Since we usually billed clients for the hours worked on their account, like a lawyer or accountant, everyone filled-out time sheets. I expected staff members to put in extra hours when necessary. But when everybody's hours were added up at the end of the month, I usually topped the list.

Write It Down. As mentioned earlier, I've always been a big note-taker. Wouldn't think of going into a business meeting without a ruled, letter-size pad. I would jot down all the important points covered at a meeting, and review them later. The key points would get a check mark; my action items got an arrow next to them. It was not unusual for me to fill-up 30 or more pads a year . . . which is 1,500 pages of notes!

The goal was to not clutter my mind trying to remember a lot of details. After I reviewed my notes, I'd tear off the sheets and have my assistant file them in the appropriate client or administrative file. These notes helped me maintain a busy schedule and be prepared. I might have a half-dozen or more meetings a day on different clients and subjects. Before each one, I'd do a quick review of my notes from the last meeting and know exactly where we left things.

Use a Pocket Secretary. Shortly after college, I started carrying a small spiral notebook and pen in my pants pocket. The pad had multi purposes. I could make brief notes and record business expenses. In addition, I used it to list appointments and the most important things I wanted to do each day.

Many years ago, I switched from plain, spiral notebooks to the Day-Timer pocket secretary system. There's a pre-printed mini notebook for each month, with a calendar and a two-page spread for each day. The monthly pads fit in a leather holder, which also houses a pen. They are now such a part of me that I seldom leave the house without my pocket secretary.

Be Organized. As the note-taking and pocket secretary suggest, being organized is very important to me. That applies to all areas of my life, personal as well as business. I've got files for trips . . . investments . . . expenses . . . health issues . . . important purchases . . . and lots of other topics.

I once read that we spend 20 to 30 percent of our time searching for things. The goal is to be able to find things when you want them and minimize the search time. Not just paperwork, but anything you use regularly. My closet . . . dresser . . . tool box . . . and sports equipment are all organized so I can find things fast.

To organize my desk paperwork, I use a multipocket notebook. It has separate sections for upcoming dates . . . things I want or need to do . . . things to buy or get . . . trips that are planned . . . and stuff that's waiting for action from others. The latter might include something I've ordered or are expecting a return phone call to discuss. On a weekly basis, I review the notebook and try to take action on as many items as necessary.

Trip Memos. Travel can be tiring. Think about all the details that go into a business or personal trip. You may have a limo taking you to the airport. A flight to catch. The rental car when you land. The hotel or motel where you're staying. All of which have phone numbers and confirmation numbers. Plus the addresses and phone info for clients or friends you might be seeing.

That's why I would always have my secretary do a trip memo that included all these details on one or two sheets of paper. I don't have a secretary anymore, but I've found these trip memos so valuable that I now prepare them myself.

Do It Right the First Time. As I pointed out in the Kobs & Brady chapter, there were a number of things that had to be repeated regularly. Like annual performance reviews, budget spreadsheets, and agency evaluations. Often they needed to be done when we were really busy. It was tempting to rush them.

It is better not to. If you don't spend the time to do it right the first time, you'll just have to spend extra time re-doing and revising it the next time around. It's much more efficient to make the first time the right time.

Become a Skillful Negotiator. That's another success secret I learned early-on. Closing a deal usually involves a lot of details. Often, there's one key provision that can make a big difference. Like the finder's fee bonus in my K&B employment contract. That one detail made me a lot of money.

While negotiating with Ted Bates, I used a different strategy. They wanted to acquire us as soon as possible. I was willing to sell. But I was in no hurry to do so. Bates was introducing us to clients that helped build our business and maximize our pay-out. So I purposely dragged out the negotiations long enough to make it one of the most profitable agency sales of that era.

Mind Your Shadow. There's something that follows you around, all through life, wherever you go. It's always there, like your shadow. The shadow I'm referring to is your reputation. Some say it's the most valuable thing you have.

You can't buy a reputation, you earn it. You earn it by being honest and trustworthy. By keeping your word. By treating others fairly. And by doing your job properly. Slowly, but surely, your reputation grows. Like any valuable possession, it should be handled carefully and protected.

Mnemonic Reminders. Have you ever thought of something important just before falling asleep and totally forgot about it by morning? Or walked out the door without something you really needed to take with you? The simple solution is to use some physical object to jog your memory.

If I want to take something along when I go to play tennis tonight, I might put it next to my tennis case. Or turn one of my tennis shoes around—to make me stop and think why I did that. I once tried keeping a pad and pen on my nightstand to jot down that big idea before dozing off. But it was too complicated to turn the light on and find my glasses before I could start writing. Now I just reach over to my sock drawer, remove a pair, and drop them on the floor. Come morning, I notice the out-of-place socks, which help me recall that big idea.

Always Be Doing. Thomas Jefferson once wrote: "It is wonderful how much may be done if we are always doing." I'm a big believer in keeping busy and not wasting time. I like to read while I eat or watch TV. What's known today as multitasking.

I've learned a lot by reading books and articles on time management, such as setting-up schedules and routines. For example, when household bills come in, I just put them in a drawer. Then I pay them all every other Monday night. Another important tip is to always have something with you to fill in those idle or waiting moments. If I take Nadine to a doctor appointment, I bring along some reading. I have extra work in my brief case for plane trips. And, of course, my pocket secretary is ever ready to make or review notes.

Goals and Priorities. It's easy to keep busy and still not accomplish much. That's why goal-setting is important. If you have a lot of goals or things to do, you need to prioritize them. To make sure you're starting with the biggies.

In the business world, it's not unusual to establish three- to five-year goals. From a personal standpoint, I like to set monthly goals. I do a new list at the beginning of each month, and keep it handy so I see it regularly. But I also review last month's list, and feel good about what I've accomplished.

Chip Away. Perhaps you have a goal that's pretty ambitious—in other words, one that's going to take a lot of time and effort. Maybe you've been putting-off getting started because you know it's such a big job.

There probably aren't any shortcuts. But breaking the goal down into smaller chunks and doing a little at a time adds up quickly. One of my favorite mystery authors wrote only ten pages each weekday. They've added up to over sixty books. This autobiography was completed by writing just one afternoon a week, and it got done in less than two years.

People Skills. When I first discovered how valuable this was, I thought it was unfair. How could someone who wasn't as smart as or didn't work as hard as I did, be doing so well? Simple. Their people skills were strong enough to make them stand out.

Gradually I managed to transform myself. To leave behind that shy, introverted guy who started college. To develop self-confidence. And to be able to get along with almost everyone. The key is to make others feel important by talking more about them than about yourself. You'll find that developing good people skills really makes it easier to get ahead.

Take Your Work, Not Yourself, Seriously. We all deal with a lot of serious stuff in life, including our jobs. But I don't believe in taking yourself too seriously. You need to be able to laugh and have fun along the way.

If your job or home life is putting you under a lot of pressure, find something to relieve the stress. What works for me is reading a chapter or two of a good mystery. Or going to a ball game. People often criticize baseball as a slow-moving sport. Maybe that's why I find it relaxing.

Fond Memories: The staff parties at Kobs & Brady. We believed in working hard and playing hard. When we went out drinking, I wasn't the big boss. I was just one of the guys. Staff members knew I liked to have fun . . . and could take some kidding, as well as dish it out.

Lessons Learned. Everyone is different. This chapter is about what worked for me. My success secrets may or may not work for you. I just hope you'll experiment with ideas like these and find some that work equally well for you.

14

Extra Innings
Some Important Leftovers

I've already written 13 chapters and more than forty thousand words. Still have some leftovers. Things that didn't fit neatly into the preceding chapters. I'm including them here in no particular order.

Important Things. The greatest things in life are not things. Material possessions are nice, and I enjoy my share of them. But it's easy to put too much emphasis on them and get spoiled.

I was pleased many years ago when Nadine got me a Rolex watch for our anniversary. It was self-winding. But it wasn't as accurate as I wanted. I finally put it in my keepsake drawer and switched to a Swiss Army watch that keeps perfect time and was a fraction of the cost.

Reminds me of a magazine article that showed the tangible possessions of average families in thirty countries around the world. The photo crew moved each family's belongings outside in front of their homes. What a contrast the pictures were. A poor African family would have a few pots and utensils outside a mud hut . . . while a U.S. family would have their cul-de-sac filled with household furnishings and appliances.

Family and Friends. These are obviously more important than your possessions. Yet in earlier chapters, I've only discussed my immediate family and mentioned a few others. Sad to say, some folks are no longer with us. Like Nadine's parents and two of her siblings. Or my Uncle Herman, who had his own woodworking business and probably inspired me to become an entrepreneur.

My cousins are spread around a little, from South Bend to Georgia. We're lucky that even though we have a niece out East, all our nephews live either in the Chicago area or Phoenix area. More family members have moved to Arizona in recent years, including my in-laws, Gerald & Becky.

When it comes to friends, Nadine and I are fortunate to have so many of them. Our Progressive Dinner group started 49 years ago, before we were married. Our multi-house dinner has shrunk to a single stop, but we still get together every year around Christmas.

Other good friends include former neighbors, like Ruth and Carl Koenemann, . . . those we met through Inverness Golf Club . . . people we worked with or travelled with . . . and the tennis players I compete with both in Chicagoland and Scottsdale. You know someone is a good friend when you haven't seen them in months, or even years, and can pick-up right where you left off.

Health and Check-Ups. Despite being left with a heart murmur from my rheumatic fever, I've been able to play tennis and softball.

Also, I guess my metabolism is better than my appetite because I've never put on a lot of weight. So I didn't see any need for regular doctor visits.

That changed as I reached middle age. One of the programs we promoted for Mayo Clinic was their executive check-up . . . a comprehensive physical that's usually completed in one day. I tried it in 1992, which was my first physical in 15 years. I was impressed enough to keep going back every year and soon had Nadine join me for her annual Mayo check-up.

Since then, I've only had a couple of serious medical problems. The main one started early in 2007. I felt fine, but my voice started getting hoarse a couple times a day. Mayo diagnosed the problem May 1, when I got my annual check-up. A biopsy confirmed it was Cancer on one of my vocal cords. I started daily radiation three weeks later. Eventually I had to deal with some pain and discomfort, but I managed to tolerate the radiation quite well.

I started a journal titled "The Big C Meets the Big J." As I noted when the treatments were completed, it was a humbling experience to realize how many people care about you. Hardly a day went by without getting a card, phone call, or e-mail to see how I was doing. The family certainly rallied around. And people I barely knew were praying for me.

The most touching support came from my wonderful wife. She said a number of times she wished she could do the treatments for me, so I wouldn't have to suffer. That's really what love is all about.

Pipe Smoking. I started at the U. of I. Thought it would make me look more sophisticated and attract nice-looking women. Judging by my wife, it obviously worked. I smoked a pipe for about fifty years and quit the morning of my biopsy. It wasn't as hard to quit as I thought it would be, but I still carry a pipe around in my shirt pocket.

One of my young grandsons noticed the pipe recently and asked me about it. I explained that I had to give up smoking a few years back when I got sick, but I still liked to carry a pipe around . . . and sometimes put it in my mouth. "Oh," he said, "now you just pretend you're smoking to look cool." That's about it!

Making the Right Choices. I'm far from perfect in this area, but I can think of a few instances where doing the right thing paid off. Like when I first started getting big bonuses at Stone & Adler. They were $5,000 and usually paid at the end of each fiscal year. One year the bonus was delayed for some reason and paid early the following year. A couple months later, our bookkeeper gave me another $5,000 check . . . thinking I hadn't received one yet for last year.

I told her I thought I had already been paid. She looked at her records and couldn't find anything about an earlier check. It was tempting to keep the check, but I was quite sure it was a mistake. So I insisted she double-check her records. She was embarrassed to report I was right. However, when she told Bob Stone about it, he was so impressed with my honesty that he told me to keep the check!

More recently, I was pulling out of the garage under our condo and scraped an old car that was parked next to me. I got out and checked. Sure enough, some of our tan paint was on the fender of the other car. The garage was dark. There was nobody around. It was tempting to drive away.

Then I remembered when somebody had dented Nadine's car

while she was parked at a golf club in Arizona. He had been nice enough to leave a note on the windshield, which made her feel a lot better. So I did the same and left a note on the old car's windshield with my name and phone number. Don't know why, but the owner never bothered to call. I guess I was lucky it didn't cost me anything. But I know I slept a lot better that night.

My Toughest Lesson. Some things are easier said than done. I've often told our kids to enjoy every day and live life to the fullest. It's been tough for me to do that. It seems like I was always trying to get things done, always trying to get ready for the future.

For many years I kept an attractive photo on my office wall. The saying under the picture was: "Life is a Journey, not a Destination." It helped remind me to not wait for the future.

Smile a While. We all have to deal with a lot of heavy stuff. But life's a lot more fun, when you have fun with it. I've always enjoyed kidding and teasing my grandsons . . . probably because I'm still a kid at heart.

When I was younger, I tried a few practical jokes that back-fired. Like sending out *phony* wedding invitations to the family, without any warning . . . which made them think Nadine was pregnant and we had to move up the wedding date. Some family members didn't think that was too funny.

But, overall, it's nice to enjoy some fun and games. Who else do you know who would open his first business on April Fool's Day? Or try to out-do his grandsons with an annual Halloween costume?

Religion and Prayers. Even though I'm a fallen-away Catholic and part-time Lutheran, I have a good relationship with God. Suppose you could say I believe in God more than I believe in practicing religion.

I always say a prayer when I go to bed at night and reflect on some of that day's activities. On a recent trip with my son, I noticed that Ken does the Sign of the Cross before take-offs and landings. For as long as I can remember, I've said a brief prayer before take-offs. I ask God to watch over my personal (and business) family members until I rejoin them . . . .and "should anything happen to me, please take good care of all my loved ones for me."

I had never read the Bible until a few years ago. It took me two years to finish, and I found it fascinating. Last fall, I joined Nadine in going to a weekly Bible class taught by Tim Hetzner. He's a great teacher and really makes the Bible come alive.

You Don't Know Me. Here are a few tidbits that even some of my family members don't know about me. My lucky number is 44, which comes from my first Cubs hero, Phil Cavarretta. Was it destiny that my future wife lived in Villa Park at 144 S. Michigan? And my first sports car was a Porsche 944?

Even though most of my hair bailed out on me years ago, I've never thought of myself as bald. I just have an extended forehead. So tell all the bald jokes you want; my self-esteem says they don't apply to me.

I have a phobia. It doesn't bother me to drive over bridges, but I get a little nervous walking on them. Maybe because I've never been a good swimmer.

Don't tell my dentist this one: I've never learned how to floss my teeth. Instead I use Panasonic's Oral Irrigator. It uses a water spray to clean-out your teeth and does a better job than a toothbrush.

If I had not become an adman, I think I would have enjoyed being an architect. I'm lucky to have lived in Chicagoland, which is known for its great architecture and magnificent skyscrapers.

Would you believe that a baseball fan like me turned down a last-minute ticket to Game 6 of the 1993 World Series? We were at a DMA convention dinner in Toronto. I had never been to a Series game. But a friend was the dinner honoree and I thought it would be disrespectful to leave. Joe Carter hit a walk-off homer that night to end the Series. At least Nadine and I got to see the victory parade the next day.

I don't have a lot of regrets, including that ball game. But I always thought it would be neat to get involved in politics. Not run for a major office. Just get on the board for my city or village. Who knows, maybe I still will.

Getting up in Years. One of my first bosses retired to Arizona. We stayed in touch and visited him in Sun City. He was probably in his eighties by then and about to go in the hospital for some tests. I called him a couple of weeks later to see how things had turned out. He said the doctor told him he was suffering from TMB. I said I'd never heard of that . . . what the heck is TMB? His reply: "Too Many Birthdays."

I'd like to think there's no such thing as too many birthdays. But as you get up in years, you have to be realistic. You may not feel old, but some of your body parts probably don't work as well as they used to. Chances are, some of your friends are in the same ballpark, age-wise. So it's not uncommon to hear about life-threatening illnesses among your peers.

You can let those things get you down. Or you can remain an

optimist. I prefer to think about all the wondrous things I've witnessed over the years . . . and all the things I hope to accomplish in the years ahead.

I spotted a tee-shirt the other day that said: "Get Revenge! Live long enough to be a problem to your children." I don't want to be a problem to anyone. But I do want to master that Pogo Stick. And don't be surprised if you see me coming around the corner next year on my Unicycle!

Appendix

THE MAN IN THE GRAY FLANNEL UNDERWEAR

A short story I wrote for a class at the University of Illinois, which was reprinted in the March 1960 issue of *Chaff*, a campus humor magazine. It's a parody of a popular contemporary novel about the ad business.

"Will you be home for supper, dear?" Helen yelled through the window as Greg dashed for the station.

"I don't know, honey . . . I'll have to call you later" he yelled back over his shoulder.

He scampered wildly through the station, knocking over three paperboys and one little old lady selling flowers. The familiar **"Alllll Aboooaarrddd"** sounded as he burst through the gate toward the train. By the time he reached his train, its smokestack was belching a thick, black smoke and its wheels had begun to move forward with a rhythmic **"C H U G—A—L U G . . . . CHUG-A-LUG . . . .Chug-A-Lug."**

The train was just starting to pick up speed as Greg caught the last car and swung aboard. For a couple of minutes he just hung on to the guard rails gasping for breath like a goldfish out of the bowl. Finally, he pulled himself up, straightened his tie, and scratched himself. He really couldn't help it—scratching himself—his underwear itched.

Unlike the popular conception of advertising men, Greg Dodson didn't wear a gray flannel business suit—just gray flannel under-wear. It wasn't that he enjoyed wearing gray flannel underwear . . . actually it got to be pretty uncomfortable this time of year . . . the hot July sun and all. Greg really did not have any choice in the mat-ter because Fruit-of-the-Loom, who made the long underwear, was one of his accounts and they insisted that employees of their adver-tising agency use their product. When Greg had first started wearing his long gray flannels, he had itched and scratched until his whole body had broken-out into one big rash. Luckily, his agency also had Ivory Soap as an account, so before lone, Greg's skin was 99 and 44/100 percent pure again.

Greg Dodson made his way to the club car, and firmly entrenched himself at the bar. As usual, the club car was quite crowded. The suburban commuters always seemed anxious to wash their breakfast down with some liquid refreshment. Some of them must have had awfully big breakfasts, because it seemed to take quite a few drinks to wash them down. Greg was one of those heavy drinkers. After all, as an advertising man, he had a reputation to uphold. It has been rumored that a good ad man can down six or seven martinis on the morning commuter train, but not Greg. Six or seven Manhattans, yes, but not martinis. He just happened to like cherries better than olives.

Anyway, with his inimitable sense of timing, Greg had just downed his seventh manhattan as the train chug-a-lugged into Grand Central Station. His attaché case in hand, Greg trudged up the station stairs, eagerly anticipating another day of creative endeavor. From the station it was just two short blocks to that most infamous of all thoroughfares—Madison Avenue, U.S.A. Commonly referred to as "ad alley" or "ulcer gulch," this was the natural habitat of the hidden persuaders. Here worked the men who made you aware that breakfast cereal snapped, crackled, and popped . . . who made you wonder where the yellow went . . . who informed you that excess stomach acid can burn a hole in a handkerchief. As Greg turned on to Madison Avenue, he unconsciously straightened his shoulders. After a quick glance around to see if anyone was watching him . . . he scratched. The gray flannel underwear still itched.

Greg was almost to the office when he recalled that he was out of cigarettes. He entered the drugstore on the first floor of his building and went up to the cigarette counter.

"A package of cigarettes, please," Greg said. Instead of mentioning the name of the brand he wanted, he began to hum the Marlboro jingle . . . the melody that goes along with "You get a lot to like with a Marlboro—filter, flavor, flip-top box." This was another of his firm's accounts; one of the more successful ones at that. An independent research firm had reported last week that 94% of all TV viewers had placed the Marlboro song among their top ten favorite jingles. However, the girl behind the cigarette counter apparently had never heard the jingle.

"What kind of cigarettes do you wish, mister?" she asked in her best Brooklynese accent.

"The one with the filter, flavor, and flip-top box," Greg answered, still hopeful the girl would recognize the slogan.

"Look, mister, we've got about two dozen different filter cigarettes . . . three or four of them come in flip-top-boxes . . . and they all have some flavor or other. I haven't got time to stand here playing guessing games!"

By this time some other people, anxious to be waited on, had gathered behind Greg, so he sheepishly asked for a package of Marlboros. As he walked away he heard the salesgirl mumbling something about all ad men being "just plain nuts."

Undaunted, Greg took the self-service elevator to the 13th floor . . . which was completely devoted to the spacious quarters of Hickenlooper, Elfman, Longfellow, and Lewis. As you may know, it is common practice in the industry to refer to multi-name ad agencies by the first letters of each name. Thus, J. Walter Thompson is known as JWT . . . Batten, Barton, Durstine, and Osborn is known as BBDO . . . and Hickenlooper, Elfman, Longfellow, and Lewis is known as HELL. You can imagine the fun the trade journals had with their acronym. When Frigidaire recently switched its advertising agency from Ogilvy, Benson, and Mather to Hickenlooper, Elfman, Longfellow, and Lewis, the headline in *Advertising Age* proclaimed:

OBM Loses Another Account, Frigidaire goes to HELL!

The double doors facing the elevator on the 13th floor were neatly lettered with the agency's full name . . . no acronym there. It was these double doors that Greg passed through each morning as he entered HELL, and this particular day was no exception.

"Good morning, Mr. Dodson," the receptionist said as she looked up from her nails, which she was busy filing.

"Let's hope so, Miss Gardner," Greg said, smiling the impish little smile he had seen Jack Lemmon use in the movie where he played an advertising executive.

Greg walked down the hall . . . past the exclusive washroom with its gold doorknob and gold keyhole . . . to his own office. In his outer office, his secretary was reading the morning newspaper. She looked up and smiled and Greg nodded. He could hear her saying something about what a nice day it was as he closed the door to his inner office behind him. With a sigh of relief, he dropped his attaché case alongside his desk and tossed his suit coat on a chair. Absent-mindedly, he scratched.

At 34 years of age, Greg Dodson was a successful ad man. It was rather ironic, too, because none of his college professors thought he would amount to anything. He had flunked out of the Engineering, Liberal Arts, and Commerce curriculums before he decided to study Advertising. He didn't do very well in Advertising either, but he managed to stay in school long enough to get a degree. That year, Hickenlooper, Elfman, Longfellow, and Lewis was looking for an enterprising young copywriter.

Enterprising young copywriters happened to be in short supply that year, so they hired Greg Dodson instead. He started out as an unheralded, inconspicuous member of HELL's large copywriting department and ten years later he was still an unheralded, incon-spicuous member of HELL's large copywriting department. Then he came up with the idea for Marlboro Cigarettes new advertising cam-paign . . . and both Marlboro and Greg became famous.

Before the advertising campaign was begun, Marlboros had been smoked mainly by men. Greg's strategy was to create a dainty, femi-nine image for the product that would attract the large market of women smokers. In each ad Greg showed a sexy, female siren smok-ing a Marlboro—and here's the clincher—each girl had a scar on her hand. Before long everyone in the ad industry was talking about the Marlboro women and their scars.

Seemingly sparked by the success of this campaign, Greg swept on to even greater success . . . creating the man in the Hathaway shirt, who always wore a Lone Ranger type mask as an identifying trademark.

When this campaign also became famous throughout the industry, Hickenlooper, Elfman, Longfellow, and Lewis had no choice but to make Greg Dodson head of the agency's creative department. Not only did this mean an increase in pay for Greg, but a private office and his own silver-plated key to the executive washroom (only Messrs. Hickenlooper, Elfman, Longfellow, and Lewis had gold-plated keys).

Such was the successful career Greg had behind him as he stood in his office, still scratching his gray flannel underwear. Just then his secretary buzzed him on the intercom.

"Mr. Hickenlooper called earlier, sir," she said when he flipped-on the intercom. "He wanted me to remind you that the Fruit-of-the-Loom people will be here this afternoon for that meeting about their new ad campaign. You hadn't forgotten, had you, Mr. Dodson?"

"How could I forget," he sighed.

It really was pretty hard to forget about the new Fruit-of-the-Loom campaign . . . wearing their itchy, old, flannel underwear served as a constant reminder. But in spite of being constantly reminded, Greg still hadn't come up with a good idea for the campaign. Fruit-of-the-Loom was pretty dissatisfied with its last campaign. There actually wasn't anything wrong with the last campaign, but the company's sales had been slipping and its advertising got the blame. Unless the agency could present a spectacular campaign idea this afternoon, Hickenlooper, Elfman, Longfellow, and Lewis would probably lose the account. And if they did, Greg would probably lose his job, key to the executive washroom and all . . . for such is the fickleness of success in the advertising business.

For two solid weeks, Greg had tried to come up with a winning idea. Out of desperation he had even considered changing the product—suggesting that Fruit-of-the-Loom market long underwear in soft, pastel colors instead of that drab gray. Or that they replace that button-down flap in the back with a more modern, zippered flap. Finally, as a last resort, he had asked the research department to do a study on long underwear. It would cover the usual questions . . . why do people buy the product . . . how is it worn . . . and how do they feel about the product. He hoped he would get some ideas from it. At any rate, it was his last hope.

Greg looked at his watch . . . just a little after ten. He buzzed the research department.

"Hello, research here."

"Hi, is Harvey there?"

"No, Mr. Wilkens isn't in yet, sir."

"What time do you expect him?...this is Greg Dodson . . . he was supposed to have a long underwear report ready for me this morning."

"Oh yes, Mr. Dodson . . . that's why he's late . . . he stayed last night to finish it up and left it on my desk. I was going to bring it over after I finish my coffeebreak."

"I would appreciate it if you drop it off whenever it's convenient for you . . . nothing really urgent about it . . . JUST MY JOB, THAT'S ALL."

A few minutes after he slammed down the phone, Greg was staring at a three-inch thick report, the cover of which read: **Analysis of Psychological and Physiological Consumer Motivation**

Regarding the Purchase and Utilitarian Values of Male Undergarments.

It was about an hour later, when Greg had penetrated about an inch deep into the report, that his secretary buzzed him on the intercom again.

"Aren't you going out to lunch today, Mr. Dodson?"

"No, I don't think so . . . maybe you could bring me some lunch back when you go and I'll drink it here at my desk."

"Will one shaker-full be enough?"

"Better make it two, Mary, this report is awfully dry."

By five minutes to two, Greg had finished the two shakersful of Manhattans and the remaining two inches of the long underwear report. With the report and a pad of scratch paper under his arm, he strode down the hall toward the conference room . . . his eyes slightly glassy, but lit up as only a great idea could light them.

Like most business meetings, this one was pretty dull. A few months ago Greg used to become bored at a dull meeting like this, but by now he had learned to amuse himself in various ways. While Greg was so amusing himself, the other executives were discussing various ideas for Fruit-of-the-Loom's long underwear campaign.

Mr. Hickenlooper had suggested the use of testimonial ads. Because adult Westerns were currently popular, he recommended that Western movie stars like Roy Rogers and Gene Autry be used to endorse the product. In general, Mr. Elfman agreed with him . . . but he felt it would be better to get an endorsement from Huckleberry Hound or other cartoon stars. Mr. Longfellow felt it would be best to advertise on American Bandstand and in college newspapers to try and develop a younger market for long underwear.

Mr. Lewis hadn't said much of anything because he had been

asleep most of the meeting. He did mumble something once about skywriting, but nobody paid any attention to him.

Finally, the unhappy client trio from Fruit-of-the-Loom had rejected every suggestion and they all turned hopefully toward Greg. He was slouched down pretty far in his chair and for a few seconds, he pretended to be deep in thought. Then he sat up abruptly, every eye in the room watching him.

"Gentlemen, this is kind of off the top of my head, but it's supported by a rather extensive report from our research department. If you don't mind, I'd like to run my idea up the flagpole and see it anyone salutes it.

"As I see it, gentlemen, the men of America are presently very frustrated individuals. They would prefer to be back in the days of cavemen, when a man was well-dressed with just a bear skin and didn't have to worry about shirts, ties, cuff links, pants, suit coats, vests, shoes, socks, hats, and so on. They would much prefer the ruggedness of the American Indian, who wore only a loin cloth . . . in fact, they . . . ."

"Are you suggesting that we start making loin cloths instead of underwear?" interrupted the president of Fruit-of-the-Loom, a worried look covering his face.

"No, sir, I'm not. But I am suggesting a way to give your product an image that will capitalize on the way the modern man feels. Check this idea—men secretly long to do away with clothes, to parade around nude or half-nude . . . right? So we do ads that show a man walking around in only his Fruit-of-the-Loom long underwear . . . but he's always walking around somewhere among normally dressed people. And the headline could read something like this: 'I wish . . . ' no, 'I dreamt . . . I dreamt I went to the ballgame in my Fruit-of-the-Loom underwear.' To every man who reads this ad it represents a beautiful example of wish fulfillment . . . he pictures himself as the guy in the underwear ad, remembers your name, and buys the product. How about that?"

No answer came from anyone . . . just silence. Everybody in the conference room sat in stunned silence as the idea sunk in, then suddenly the silence was shattered by spontaneous cries of "Hurray! Hurray!"

"Let's get started on it right away . . . ."

"The greatest idea anyone has had since the Marlboro woman. . . ."

"Our underwear sales will stop slipping when these ads break. . . ."

"It's even better than using Huckleberry Hound!"

"Nobody else could have come up with a big idea like this . . . ."

"Aren't we going to use skywriting?"

Greg just leaned back contentedly, and since nobody was watching him, he scratched. "Maybe I'll even be able to stop wearing this damn, itchy underwear from now on," he thought.

So after another trying day in the life of the man in the gray flannel underwear, Greg Dodson caught the afternoon club car for home. As you can probably guess, the Fruit-of-the-Loom campaign was a tremendous success and every advertiser in the country wanted to switch his advertising to Hickenlooper, Elfman, Longfellow, and Lewis. Which just goes to show—if you drink enough Manhattans, every advertiser in the country will go to HELL.

STOP THE PLANE, I Want to Get Off!

Early in 1982 I was on a flight to Miami with an attempted hijacking. I was welcomed back to the office a couple days later with a party, sombrero, and lots of questions. So I wrote a tongue-in-cheek staff memo, which was later reprinted in the April 5, 1982 issue of *Advertising Age*.

TO: **K & B Staff**
FROM: **Jim Kobs**
SUBJECT: **All in a Day's Work?**

As I think you know by now, I was on the United Airlines flight earlier this week with a hijacker who wanted to go to Cuba. I hope none of you ever has to go through something like that. But just in case, here's what it's like.

I was meeting Howard and Connie in Miami for an important new business presentation. They took most of the stuff for the meeting, but I was bringing all the creative materials in a big art case. Naturally, I couldn't take a chance on checking it . . . so I charmed the stewardess into letting me bring it on board.

The flight started out quite normally. The usual plastic airline food, stewardesses with plastic smiles, etc. We were about 45-minutes out of Miami when we got wind that something was going on. The stews just said there's some nut on board, like it was no big deal. So I settled back to have an after-dinner drink, while I finished preparing my notes for the Miami meeting.

All of a sudden, the plane started dropping altitude fast—and the stewardesses said they had to pick up all the trays and glasses. I kind of suspected what was going on. And since I had only taken one sip of my drink before it was cleared away, I knew I didn't like the guy.

A few minutes later, the pilot announced we were going to Cuba and had been cleared to land in Havana. I told the stewardess I really didn't want to go to Cuba . . . while they are well-known for their cigars, I've never heard of any good Cuban pipe tobacco. She thought I was kidding!

At this point, things started to get a little scary. The hijacker was at the very rear of the plane, near the washrooms, so all the coach passengers kept coming upfront by me to use the first-class washroom. Besides that, the hijacker kept flicking his Bic (see what those TV commercials do) at this glass bottle with a wick coming out of it. Maybe the airlines will have to put in glass detectors to stop this kind of thing.

One of the co-pilots started back with a fire extinguisher in hand, but decided it wasn't safe to go any closer to the hijacker than the front of the coach section.

After a few more minutes, you could see lights in the distance, like we were approaching a city. The guy next to me said he didn't think we could be to Cuba yet . . . that the pilot had probably circled around over the Everglades and was coming into Miami or Fort Lauderdale. I wondered why they were playing "trick the hijacker" when he probably still had hundreds of lights left in his Bic. I also said a few silent prayers.

All of a sudden we landed—and stopped abruptly on the outskirts of some airport. The stewardesses started chanting: "Yeah, Cuba . . . yeah, Cuba" and a few of the passengers joined in. If you're playing "trick the hijacker," you might as well go all the way.

At this point, the pilot rushed out of the cockpit and headed back toward the hijacker. As soon as the pilot passed them, some people in the front of the plane apparently decided they had seen this movie, and it was time to get off. I'm not sure if they were just tired of playing "trick the hijacker," were scared the plane would blow up, or had a tight connecting flight.

In any case, the guy next to me practically pushed me out of my seat toward the exit in the front galley. He turned out to be a real leader because he was the only guy on board who had been listening to the safety demonstration at the beginning of the flight, and he actually knew where our closest exit was. I had enough presence of mind to grab my attaché case, but I had no chance to get the art case with the creative presentation.

The next thing I knew, I was sliding down this inflatable emergency ramp with my pipe in one hand and my attaché case in the other (some photographer really missed a good picture!).

About 25 to 30 people took the emergency exit route. Once on the ground, somebody kept moving us back farther and farther from the plane. I think I'll always remember standing in that field with my attaché case in hand . . . trying to remember who it was that first told me there'd never be a dull moment in the ad agency business.

Then it dawned on me that the whole creative presentation was still on the plane with the hijacker and most of the passengers . . . .

What if he found out we were really in Florida and they couldn't find a room for him in-season? Would he make them take off for Havana?

Would Fidel Castro really appreciate our direct marketing presentation? How would I ever explain to my creative people that all the great layouts and copy they had worked so hard on, never quite made it to the meeting? I thought it would be easier to rescue the presentation than it would be to explain.

But as I started back toward the plane, I suddenly saw some big guys drag the hijacker off and introduce him to the airport security people.

After that, it was all downhill. The glad-to-be-alive passengers were bussed to the terminal . . . happily agreed to be locked-up for an hour in an FBI debriefing room without phones or washrooms (I knew I should have gone before the coach passengers pushed their way upfront) . . . and graciously consented to media interviews on the way out.

In the debriefing room I talked to the passenger who had tackled the hijacker. He was built like one of the Bears football players. He told me he had slept though almost the whole flight . . . woke up when we were landing . . . heard people chanting Cuba . . . decided it was this nut's fault . . . and threw a body tackle at him.

Once we were safe inside the terminal, there was a lot of good-natured kidding around. The best line I heard was from my former seat-mate. He said: "I wasn't positive we were in Miami until we got in the airport and everyone around us was speaking Spanish. Then I knew it was Miami."

In retrospect, this was one of those experiences that's a little funnier now than it was then. Seriously, though, if any of you need to schedule me into client meetings in the near future, please allow time for me to get there on Amtrak. Have you ever heard of anyone hijacking a train to Cuba?

Index